STARMONT STUDIES IN LITERARY CRITICISM NO. 10
ISSN 0737-1306

STEPHEN KING
as
Richard Bachman

MICHAEL R. COLLINGS

☆ Starmont House, Inc. ☆
Mercer Island, Washington
1985

Library of Congress Cataloging In Publication Data

Collings, Michael R.
  Stephen King as Richard Bachman.

  (Starmont studies in literary criticism ; #10)
  Bibliography: p. 161-166.
  Includes index.
  1. King, Stephen, 1947-   --Criticism and interpretation. 2. Horror tales, American -- History and criticism. I. Title. II. Series: Starmont studies in literary criticism (Mercer Island, Wash.) ; #10.
  PS3561.I483Z6283   1985   813´.54   85-2832
  ISBN 0-930261-01-1
  ISBN 0-930261-00-3 (pbk.)

Published and copyright © 1985 by Starmont House, Inc. All rights reserved. International copyrights reserved in all countries. No part of this book may be reproduced in any form, except for brief passages quoted in reviews, without expressed written consent of the publisher. For information address Starmont House, Inc., P.O. Box 851, Mercer Island WA 98040. Cover design by Stephen E. Fabian.

Second Printing --- January 1986

Michael R. Collings, an Associate Professor of English at Pepperdine University in Malibu, California, has written Piers Anthony: A Reader´s Guide and Brian W. Aldiss: A Reader´s Guide, both for Starmont House. He has also published critical articles on Science Fiction and Fantasy, as well as short fiction, and poetry.

DEDICATION AND ACKNOWLEDGMENTS

To Stephen King, for being Richard Bachman <u>and</u> Stephen King;

To Ted Dikty of Starmont House and Rob Reginald of Borgo Press for supporting this project;

To David Engebretson, who as both student and colleague is an integral part of "Team Horror";

To Barbara Bolan of Second Edition Books for her valuable information, encouragement, advice, and well-timed laughter;

To Virginia Randolph, William Deese, and Jay Smith of Pepperdine University Library's Payson Library for help in locating materials;

To Stephanie Leonard and the staff of <u>Castle Rock</u> for their support;

Most of all to my family--to Michael-Brent, Erika, Ethan, and Kendra, for putting up with an absent (and absent-minded) Daddy. And to Judith, who proofread the manuscript while bed-ridden and gave me unfailing love and support at a time when she needed even more than she could give.

Michael R. Collings

Thousand Oaks, CA
May Day, 1985

CONTENTS

Chapter I: A History For Richard Bachman. . . .1
Chapter II: Genre, Theme, and Image in
    Richard Bachman 9
Chapter III: Rage 20
Chapter IV: The Long Walk 46
Chapter V: Roadwork 70
Chapter VI: The Running Man 92
Chapter VII: Thinner. 115
Chapter VIII: Speculations. 138
Appendix: The Bachman Novels--Synopses. . .155
List of Works Cited 159
Index 165

Chapter I

A HISTORY FOR RICHARD BACHMAN

On February 9, 1985, Stephen King announced that since 1977 he had published five novels under the pseudonym "Richard Bachman," the most recent of which, Thinner, was already moving toward best-seller status.

For some collectors, the announcement was no surprise; they had suspected a connection for years. Others became convinced in the last year, with the publication of Thinner. Bob and Phyllis Weinberg noted in catalogues as early as November, 1984, that Bachman was a pseudonym for King; Lloyd Currey's catalogue carried a similar comment (Fantasy Mongers 5; Collins 15).

All of this developed in spite of King's denials. In a letter dating from May 1981, King stated that "the rumor has gotten around that I am Richard Bachman, but it's not true. I know him and I believe he lives in Connecticut--as I recall, he was a surly fellow." A little over a year later, in August, 1982, King wrote, "I'm not 'Richard Bachman', but I know who he is, and I can't tell. Professional ethics, and all that!"

As Thinner drew a wider readership, however, not even explicit denials could scotch the rumors. A review of Thinner in Fantasy Mongers commented:

> I don't know who the guy in the author's picture is, but I do know Stephen King when I read him, and this novel is pure King in style, syntax, character development, dialog, plot structure, humor, gross outs, and even in technical mistakes. (5)

The reviewer continued to argue that because Thinner did not carry King's name on the cover, it ran the risk of getting lost among the many horror novels published in 1984, particularly when competing against novels by F. Paul Wilson and King himself. By the end of his discussion, the reviewer simply refers to King as author: "As Steve has said so many times, if he can't scare you, then he'll gross you out, and he manages to do both equally well in Thinner" (5).

The increasing speculation culminated with Steve Brown's researches at the Library of Congress, which in turn led to a discussion with King and King's subsequent interview with the Bangor Daily News: Stephen King is Richard Bachman, a fact heretofore known for certain only by Robert DiForio, NAL Chairman and chief executive officer; Elaine Koster, NAL's executive vice-president and publisher; and the NAL contract lawyer responsible for the paperwork ("Bachman Revealed" 43). The Fogler Library at the University of Maine at Orono and the Bangor Public Library had at one time listed the Bachman books under King's name; in 1984, King requested that they not so file his books, but did not acknowledge the pseudonym. But now the news was official.

King's readers reacted almost immediately. Within hours, they deluged booksellers and dealers with requests for Bachman novels, only to discover that three were already out-of-print: Rage, written partially while King was still in high school and thus a pre-Carrie attempt; Roadwork; and The Running Man. The fifth, Signet's The Long Walk, completed while he was a freshman in college (a second pre-Carrie novel) was still in print with NAL.

By February 14, however, a telephone call to New American Library in New York revealed that on the previous Monday, a nationwide chain had purchased all of the publisher's copies of The Long Walk. For all practical purposes, that novel too was now out of print. Copies of the English editions remained available through New English Library, but locating them became more and more difficult. In a sense, the auction has begun; at a fan conference in April, a first-edition Signet paperback was priced at $40.00; by May, one book dealer was offering paperback first editions for $100.00.

Shortly after King's interview, NAL announced a forthcoming trade paperback, omnibus edition of Rage, The Long Walk, The Running Man, and Roadwork, to be published under the Plume imprint with an introduction by King. This meant that in several months, presumably in the fall, King's readers could enjoy four new novels, following closely on the heels of The Talisman (with Peter Straub), and Skeleton Crew, a collection of short fiction scheduled for publication in the summer of 1985.

In the meantime, however, several questions remained. Why had King resorted to a pseudonym? And why one so completely developed that he invented a persona to fit Bachman's name, so pervasive that NAL included a dust jacket photograph of "Bachman" (actually Richard A. Manuel, a Minnesota real estate agent and friend of King's agent, Kirby McCauley ["Bachman Revealed" 43]), crediting the photograph to "Claudia Bachman," the same "Claudia Inez Bachman" to whom the novel is dedicated.

The answer, King says, is simple. As he told the Bangor Daily News, "It's been a chronic problem not wanting to over publish." According to Castle Rock: The Stephen King Newsletter, he was encouraged to limit publication under the name "Stephen King" to one or two novels a year (#3, 1). His reaction seems justified, in view of his dedication to writing, what some have referred to as his compulsion to write. As Douglas Winter notes in Stephen King: The Art of Darkness, King began writing seriously at the age of seven or eight, submitting stories to science fiction magazines within two or three years. By the age of twenty, he had sold his first short story, completed one novel-length manuscript, and garnered his first rejection of a "true novel" (xv-xvii). By the time Carrie was published in 1974, King had completed at least four novels, including what would later appear as Rage and The Long Walk.

In the next ten years, he published eleven

novels: 'Salem's Lot (1975), The Shining (1977), The Stand (1978), The Dead Zone (1979), Firestarter (1980), Cujo (1981), Christine (1983), Cycle of the Werewolf (1983), Pet Sematary (1983), The Talisman (1984: with Peter Straub), and The Eyes of the Dragon. In addition, he published four volumes of stories: Night Shift (1978); The Dark Tower: The Gunslinger (1982), a compilation of tales originally published in Fantasy & Science Fiction between 1978 and 1982; Creepshow (1982), a comic-book adaptation of five stories; and Different Seasons (1982), a collection of four novellas. Add to that impressive record a number of uncollected stories, his study of horror as a genre in Danse Macabre (1981), scores of articles and interviews, film versions of six novels and one short story, plus increasing critical attention, including Winter's premier full-length study The Reader's Guide to Stephen King (1982) . . . and it becomes evident that King was not only prolific but threatening to become overly so.

Responses to his fiction, almost to his mystique, were two-fold. Readers seemed unable to get enough King. Fans and collectors vied for first editions of his books; signed, numbered, limited first editions of some run as high as $450. One of the twenty-six special limited editions (second issue) of Firestarter, bound in asbestos and painted with aluminum paint (presumably in case Charlie McGee should turn her pyrotechnic abilities on the reader) costs a mere $1800.

His children's novel, The Eyes of the Dragon (1984), was published in a limited run of 1250 at an initial price of $120.00. According to the Philtrum Publishing Company , all orders would be placed in a lottery, the first 1000 drawn to receive copies of the novel. To increase the intrinsic value of the book, Philtrum further stipulated that the novel would not be reprinted until 1987. The implications were clear: If you want to read The Eyes of the Dragon, read now. As of March, 1985, copies of the novel--when available at all--were bringing prices up to $400; two months later, one dealer was asking $800.

Other readers responded similarly, if on lower financial strata. <u>Carrie</u>, King's first paperback sale, is now in its fortieth printing from Signet. <u>The Talisman</u>, perhaps the most eagerly awaited fantasy novel in publishing history, set records with its first hardcover printing of 600,000 copies, priced at $18.95; even then, a second printing was necessary. There are now at least 780,000 copies out; a recent <u>Newsweek</u> review placed the total at over 1,000,000.

And it is increasingly difficult to locate many earlier King stories and novels. "The Monkey" (1980) and "The Raft" (1982) first appeared as pull-out booklets in <u>Gallery</u>. Recently, while trying to locate copies of the stories, I discovered that although the issues were available (complete with exotic photographs) in used-book stores, the King stories had been removed. Apparently King was more popular than the centerfolds. Nor was it unusual to discover that in a full run of <u>Heavy Metal</u>, for instance, the only issue missing would be July, 1981, which contained a revised version of King's "The Blue Air Compressor."

Even more indicative of his popularity is the scarcity of issues of <u>The Magazine of Fantasy and Science Fiction</u> containing stories later collected in <u>The Dark Tower</u>, second editions of which now cost as much as $90.00. Readers hoping to beat that price by locating the stories in individual issues face almost immediate disappointment. Even copies of <u>Thinner</u>, which were readily visible through early February at Daltons and Waldenbooks in Los Angeles, had disappeared by February 22, to be replaced in March by a second print run and later by a third and fourth printing.

Many critics, on the other hand, reacted quite differently. Instead of welcoming new King novels, many have, over the past few years, become increasingly hostile, viewing King as little more than a glorified hack, churning out what Leslie Fiedler calls eroticized Dark Fantasy. King, Fiedler states, "has indeed finally become--in his own words--a 'brand name' like Vaseline or Coca Cola" or, in Fiedler's own words, the "master of horror schlock" (7-9). Similarly, in spite of the commercial success of King's *Christine* and Peter Straub's *Floating Dragon*, King recently said, concerning *The Talisman*,

> I don't know what the critics are going to make of it. When we started the project, I thought that, critically, we would be destroyed. I don't know if that's true any longer, because I think the book is strong. But one bellwether is that, in their "Best and Worst of the Year" article, *People* magazine put *Christine* and *Floating Dragon* in the same little review in their "Worst" section and said, "Watch out for these guys, they have written two of the worst novels of 1983 on their own, and in 1984, they are teaming up to do a book together." (Winter, "Quest" 68)

King's fears have in part been justified. There is a general sense within the media that *The Talisman*, for example, is but another "King of the Month" novel, and obviously someone who produces so many (and such long) novels lies outside of literature. Other critics simply refuse to mention King's name in other than menacing undertones; what good, they imply, could come from a writer who has written so many novels and earned so much money.

With critical attitudes as bleak as these, it seems small wonder that King elected to publish five additional novels as he did, under another name, thus avoiding the inevitable charges against them. His tactics, while frustrating to the fan, seem to have produced results. While the first four novels remained in the background, *Thinner* steadily moved upward in sales in spite of the notorious recalcitrance of Richard Bachman to speak about his novels or even to be seen.

In essence, King has shown that his works can succeed with or without the magic of his "brand name" on the label. And he has avoided the censure of those who believe that his acknowledged output represented a supererogation of authorial privilege; in the best of all possible worlds, no one should be as prolific as King, or as successful.

Such attitudes, of course, ignore two important points about King. The first is that although a young man, he has served a rigorous apprenticeship to his craft. As King notes in <u>Night Shift</u>, he has a salable obsession; he writes essentially for himself, while touching chords of fear and terror in his readers as well (xiii). But his success did not come easily.

The second point is that he has continued to work and to write. Although King has said in interviews that he writes slowly, 1800 to 2200 words per day (Modderno), Winter notes that he tries to write "every day except for his birthday, Christmas, and the Fourth of July" (<u>Art of Darkness</u> 13). His dedication, coupled with a visual and visceral imagination and a lucid style, has resulted in novel after novel, story after story.

As a result of his concentrated effort, King is now indeed a "brand name," a household word for horror; and that may in fact be the most important reason why the Bachman novels did not initially appear under his name. In <u>The Art of Darkness</u>, Winter says that King´s first use of a pseudonym, "John Swithen," resulted from <u>Cavalier</u>´s insistence that the name <u>Stephen King</u> be associated explicitly with horror; the Swithen story, "The Fifth Quarter" (<u>Cavalier</u>, April 1972) is a crime story. Similarly, with the exception of <u>Thinner</u>, the Bachman novels relate only tangentially to the supernatural horror King´s readers expect and demand: haunted houses, haunted cars, haunted dogs, ghosts and ghouls and things fresh from the grave. The Bachman novels suggest such elements, but rarely allow them to surface. Even in <u>Thinner</u>, much of the novel elapses before Billy Halleck accepts the "supernatural" explanation for what is happening to him: that he is the victim of a gypsy curse. As strong as the novels are, they are not "typically" Stephen King; his publishing them pseudonymously retains the sense of "King" as "brand name" for horror.

Nor is this the end of the readers' quest. Since he has now acknowledged writing under two pseudonyms, rumors of other "unknown" King novels have surfaced. Some years ago, for instance, King is supposed to have revealed that he wrote two novels, one science fiction and one occult-horror. The first, the story continues, was submitted to DAW books and rejected; the second was published. Another rumor is that King wrote two series of five novels each, one science fiction and one mystery suspense, and that all ten novels were published under false names.

More recently, a review in the April 1985 issue of <u>Fantasy Review</u> raised the issue of "John Wilson" as a pseudonym used before the publication of <u>Carrie</u> in conjunction with five erotic novels originally published by Beeline. One of the novels, <u>Love Lessons</u>, was supposed to have been reprinted by Pinetree Press. The reviewer, Helen Purcell, has "no doubt that King actually did write this book," noting that he has not yet denied writing the novels (31). Later information, however, reveals that the review was a hoax--the book, the publisher, and the reviewer were all fabrications.

These and other suppositions remain at the level of rumor, of course, some more solidly supported than others, but rumors nonetheless. The existence of such rumors is itself important. Some critics may decry King's accomplishments, just as they disparage the accomplishments of other prolific writers, but the readers do not. In spite of critical presuppositions about King, the fact remains that he answers a need in millions of readers. There is something in his writing, in his imagination, in his approaches to reality and illusion that touches responsive chords. With the addition of five acknowledged novels to his canon, he has given us new opportunities to discover and define precisely what that something might be.

Chapter II:

GENRE, THEME, AND IMAGE
IN RICHARD BACHMAN

In an article surveying the state of horror fantasy, Douglas Winter noted that "As horror fiction entered the 1980s, Stephen King was the undisputed master of the field." Winter's assessment was based on King's wide range of tones and touches, including his ability to write on "non-supernatural (but not necessarily non-horrific) themes" ("Art of Darkness" 3), as evidenced by three stories in Different Seasons.

Winter's statement is important in analyzing the Bachman novels, since they too attain to the horrific without the supernatural elements readers associate with King; only Thinner incorporates any major plot developments that could be called supernatural.

In a sense, King's decision to publish the four non-supernatural horror novels under a pseudonym is consistent with a current trend in horror fiction. Contemporary horror is a diluted phenomenon, in which internal, visceral responses, i.e., horror and terror, are occasionally overwhelmed by external, intellectual responses: fear of the bomb, of terrorism, of political conditions beyond individual control. Charles Grant, a noted author, critic, and anthologist in the field, argues that horror fiction is based ultimately on fear of the unknown; but

> The modern world is much too sophisticated for that . . . and so are we also far too educated to cringe at bumps in the night, creaking doors, ghosts, vampires, werewolves, and the wind that dances with dead leaves in the gutter. . . . If there is fear, it must be born in the real world--born of wars and

murders, muggings and insidious carcinoma. It is literal nonsense to believe otherwise. The horror/fantasy story is the dark side of Romanticism, and there is no room in the practical world for a Romantic. (7)

A comforting thought, he notes, but inaccurate. Beneath the rational lurks the irrational, the anticipation of horror (as opposed to the revulsion we experience in many "splatter" films and novels). This area of shadow, of tingling anticipation, is the proper province of horror fantasy: "those shadows over there in the corner that do not quite resolve themselves into objects familiar, that shadow formed by a coat over the back of a chair at the foot of your bed, the shadow that presses across an empty autumn street . . . the shadow that has no light to give it birth" (9).

In general, King works within the sphere of that internal horror; his novels contain elements that classify him with Poe, Lovecraft, and other practitioners of the horrific. In his Guest of Honor address at the International Conference on the Fantastic in the Arts (March 1984), King referred to the urge to "make up unreality" as

> inborn, innate, something that's sunk into the creative part of the mind like a great big asteroid full of metallic alloys, an asteroid that causes a compass needle to swing away from true north and toward it, should a compass be near. ("Dr. Seuss" 10)

Later, referring to the influence of Mary Shelley's <u>Frankenstein</u> and H. G. Wells' <u>War of the Worlds</u>, he argued that the "dreadful" appreciation he had for such "tales of science fiction and horror indicates again that compass needle turning from true north to the huge piece of alien metal buried in the earth" ("Dr. Seuss" 10-11).

The metal that most readers point to in King's novels seems alien, of the same composition as in Lovecraft or Poe, "eldritch" metal (to borrow Lovecraft´s trademark adjective), unearthly or weird but buried deep in the soil of this world. For Lovecraft, the meteor of imagination embedded itself in the eerie countryside around Arkham, Innsmouth, and the Miskatonic Valley. In Lovecraft´s "The Colour Out of Space" (1927), the image of a meteor became startlingly real, and the changes that bit of alien matter brought upon Nahum Gardner and his family on their farm west of Arkham were truly horrific. (In this context, readers might enjoy re-viewing "The Lonesome Death of Jordy Verrill," the second episode in <u>Creepshow</u>.) For Poe, the landscapes varied, subsumed under a pervasive atmosphere, as if the air itself were tainted by an alien intruder.

King frequently re-creates the landscapes and the atmospheres of Lovecraft, Poe, and others, allowing him to be included in listings such as Edward J. Zagorski´s. After discussing contributions by Mary Shelley, Edgar Allan Poe, Bram Stoker, and Robert Louis Stevenson, Zagorski continues:

> An honor roll could be made of horror-fiction writers since these masters. This list would most certainly include the familiar names of Oscar Wilde, Algernon Blackwood, H. P. Lovecraft, Daphne du Maurier, and Shirley Jackson, right on up through those still writing today, among them Ira Levin, Peter Straub, Richard Matheson, and Stephen King. (11)

Stories such as "Nona" (1978) illustrate King´s command of the genre and simultaneously acknowledge his debt to Lovecraft, Poe, and others. The story begins with a tone reminiscent of Poe´s "The Black Cat." Poe´s narrator is caught between fact and illusion, between reality and fantasy:

> For the most wild yet most homely narrative which I am about to pen, I neither expect nor solicit belief. Mad

> indeed would I be to expect it, in a case where my very senses reject their own evidence. Yet mad I am not--and very surely I do not dream. But tomorrow I die, and to-day I would unburden my soul. (247)

The remaining sentences of the opening paragraph continue the narrator's exercise in self-contradiction, as he leads into a story with little overt violence but an overwhelming sense of horror, of instant punishment and misplaced terror. Rosemary Jackson has referred to Poe's tale as a paradigmatic example of horror fiction, largely because of the narrative stance Poe assumes:

> Fantastic narratives . . . . assert that what they are telling is real . . . and then they proceed to break that assumption of realism by introducing what--within those terms--is manifestly unreal. They pull the reader from the apparent familiarity and security of the known and everyday world into something more strange, into a world whose improbabilities are closer to the realm normally associated with the marvellous. The narrator is no clearer than the protagonist about what is going on, nor about interpretation . . . . This instability of narrative is at the centre of the fantastic as a mode. Thus the circles of equivocation in Poe's stories, such as the opening of "The Black Cat." (34)

And thus the circles of equivocation in "Nona":

> I don't know how to explain it, even now. I can't tell you why I did those things. I couldn't do it at the trial, either. And there are a lot of people here who ask me about it. There's a psychiatrist who does. But I am silent.

> My lips are sealed. Except here in my
> cell. Here I am not silent. I wake up
> screaming. (187)

Beneath the facade of rationality lies madness . . . or an intrusion of horror into reality. The tone of King's sentences suggests what C. S. Lewis referred to as "realism of presentation," the idea that effective fantasy must provide the reader with as many points of contact with reality as possible to facilitate belief in the non-real. Readers almost automatically ignore the disclaimers King's narrator makes: He <u>can</u> explain what he did and why he did it . . . and he will, in the following pages. King provides sufficient clues, even within the narrow framework of this opening paragraph, telegraphing to his readers a tone and atmosphere which he carefully develops in the subsequent tale.

There is more to "Nona" than merely an introduction, however. As the tale progresses, King skillfully blends Poe and Lovecraft: Poe's obsession with things dead, Lovecraft's image of rats as external indicators of internal states, as in "The Rats in the Walls" (a story that compares nicely with King's "Graveyard Shift").

Even more explicitly, King's short story, "Crouch End," appearing as it did in Ramsey Campbell's <u>New Tales of the Cthulhu Mythos</u>, immediately leads the reader to anticipate horrors associated with Lovecraft's private mythology of the Cyclopean, buried cities of the Great Old Ones, the insanity of the <u>Necronomicon</u> of the mad Arab Abdul Alhazred, etc.

King, then, has developed a reputation for a certain kind of fiction. In the "Afterword" to <u>Different Seasons</u>, King notes that his editor, Bill Thompson, was concerned about the plot outline for <u>The Shining</u>: "<u>First</u> the telekinetic girl, <u>then</u> the vampires, <u>now</u> the haunted hotel and the telepathic kid. You're gonna get typed" (521). King's response was both typical and important: if being a "horror writer" placed him in the company of Lovecraft, Clark Ashton Smith, Frank Belknap Long, Fritz Leiber, Robert Bloch,

Richard Matheson, and Shirley Jackson . . . well, there could be worse places.

As a result, King has associated himself with a particular variety of contemporary horror literature, even filming an American Express commercial specifically designed to elicit and emphasize that relationship. At the same time, however, he has frequently explored the boundaries of that sub-genre, writing stories that touch only peripherally on the overtly horrific. The gentleness and compassion of "Do the Dead Sing?," for example, nearly obscure the fact of ghostly visitation, a fact that exists only by virtue of the hat found on Stella Flanders' frozen body. Even in the novels, he occasionally departs from the expected. <u>Cujo</u> is in one sense about a "haunted dog," but the haunting relies on rationality; the dog is hydrophobic. In spite of the fairy tale opening, Winter argues, "<u>Cujo</u> is steeped . . . in a reality that is as inescapable as it is frightening" (<u>The Art of Darkness</u> 95). The novel suggests the horrors of Poe and Lovecraft, giving us brief glimpses of a shadowy something in the dark closet, but the hints do not materialize. Instead, the novel is about unrelenting horror within the objective world we know, a world where dogs go mad and children die.

This is also the world of the Bachman novels. <u>Rage</u> is an anti-<u>Carrie</u> in which King highlights the isolation, fears, and pressures implicit in high-school society, but without telekinesis. Charlie Decker spreads sufficient destruction (physical and psychical) with only a pistol. He does not need to call a rain of stones from the skies to emphasize his point. In <u>The Long Walk</u>, King creates an extraordinary sense of horror without relying on stock devices or motifs. This horror is one of physical agony as the characters walk, increasingly aware of the meaninglessness of their suffering for themselves and for others. King uses horror imagery, and even refers to Shirley Jackson, but the novel itself is firmly grounded in reality. It is in some senses science fiction, since it is ostensibly placed in the near future; its effect, however, turns less on future speculation than on observing contemporary states. <u>Roadwork</u> focuses on one man's private battle against bureaucracy and isolation in the context of "The First Energy Crisis." <u>The Running Man</u> is again an exercise in speculative fiction. Although set in the year 2025, it criticizes contemporary political, social, and commercial realities.

Each novel contains stylistic devices and other hints as to authorship: <u>The Long Walk</u>, for example, is dedicated to King's professor, Burton Hatlen; Carrie's mother works at the Blue Ribbon laundry, as does Barton George Dawes in <u>Roadwork</u> and Stanner in "The Mangler." Only in <u>Thinner</u> does King merge style and motif with the content so recognizably his own.

Yet knowing that King wrote the Bachman novels explains a number of similarities. King has not divorced these five novels from his others; they explore many of the same themes from different perspectives. In style, theme, structure, and characterization, they are identifiably Stephen King.

Stylistically, the five novels reflect King's techniques, although to differing degrees. There is the same emphasis on realism of presentation through the constant, almost insistent use of brand names to establish the validity of the world King has chosen to explore. His prose is crisp, clear, often blunt--long a trademark in King's fiction. The language is likewise blunt, often crude, but rarely gratuitously so. King does not hesitate to use non-standard diction, but usually reserves it for specific purposes in characterization. The Bachman novels are, if anything, freer in their use of objectionable language than the novels published under King's name.

Similarly, King treats sexuality with greater openness here than in many of his other novels. Characters discuss sexuality and sex acts with less reserve; narrators present the acts in more graphic detail. In <u>Thinner</u>, in fact, sexuality lies at the base of Billy Halleck's problem, both with the gypsy and with his wife; her illicit sex act sets the plot in motion and makes irrevocable the direction of Halleck's intended revenge. Rage and The Long Walk concentrate openly and frankly on developing adolescent sexuality, as did Carrie, with the consequence that much of the text is devoted to discussions, comparisons, and denials of characters' sexual identities. Roadwork traces a disintegrating marriage through separation, isolation, and infidelity into madness and death; in this sense, it closely parallels The Shining, with the systematic destruction of relationships between Jack, Wendy, and Danny Torrance. The Running Man focuses less overtly on sexuality. Its science fictional framework in part militates against excursions into sexual practices, but the plot still hinges on a sexual relationship, as Ben Richards attempts to insure his family's security.

As in many of King's novels and short stories, however, sexuality is ambiguous. Necessary for survival, it is also destructive, particularly for adolescents not yet mature enough to cope with their own struggles and the struggles of others. Charlie Decker (Rage) and Ray Garraty (The Long Walk) each find individual outlets for their fears and frustrations, one through external violence, the other through punishing his body literally to the point of death. Characters frequently assure and reassure themselves of their "straight" sexuality. As elsewhere in King, homosexuality is both insistently derided and uncomfortably appealing; Garraty desires and fears McVries' touch. The characters' actions and the reactions of adults surrounding them are frequently referred to in sexual terms. When a Walker is shot in The Long Walk, the crowd makes a sound that "might have been a sigh or a groan or an almost sexual outletting of pleasure" (193). In sexual terms, no one is secure. Linda Halleck's impending sexual maturity helps explain her involvement in the final permutations of the gypsy's curse, just as diminishing sexuality helps shape Bart Dawes' reactions to the impending roadwork.

Sexuality transcends merely the individual, however. The Bachman novels also reflect another insistent motif in King's fiction, the disintegration or fragmentation of the family. Fathers disappear; mothers become bloated, demanding, overbearing, a direction that culminates in the semi-autobiographical 1984 story "Gramma." Children die of tumors. Fathers cannot protect them from harsh realities, from worlds where fathers run over old gypsy women. Ultimately, fathers become threats: Carl Decker describes graphically what he would do to anyone sleeping with his wife, unaware that young Charlie is listening and remembering crawling into his mother's bed after Carl left for work. Throughout Rage, Charlie refers to the Cherokee nose-job, an image that epitomizes his hatred of his father. His mother is not much better, however, with her insular attitudes. Only in Thinner (and then only briefly, before the horrific elements begin compounding) does King suggest a close family unity. In many ways, that initial closeness serves merely to enhance the final horror.

Fragmentation leads, in turn, to isolation. The central characters in each of the Bachman novels is increasingly isolated. They lose family, friends, life itself. Charlie Decker makes his own isolation, locking himself away from parents, teachers, friends, and forcing the students he imprisons in the classroom to undergo a similar isolation. Ray Garraty's isolation is even more paradigmatic; he begins the Long Walk as one in a company of a hundred. One by one, the Walkers drop out, friends become foes, until only one remains, isolated physically and emotionally from any human contact. The same pattern recurs in Roadwork, The Running Man, and Thinner, each ending with the actual or implied death of the character. There are no viable societies in these novels; individuals ultimately survive or die on their own.

Isolation in turn suggests helplessness, a final motif that unifies the Bachman novels and makes them an inherent part of King's imagined universe. In spite of everything--pain, suffering, death--no one can finally do anything. Characters become enmeshed by social pressure, politics, the external environment; they can no longer control themselves, their actions, or the actions of others. The only recourse is violence, an outlet (and motif) explored most fully in <u>The Running Man</u>, with its emphasis on social and political critique.

In addition, there are a number of minor elements that clearly connect the Bachman novels with King's larger body of works. Cancer as threat underlies much of his fiction; Billy Halleck, for example, first assumes that his weight loss is a result of cancer. Only later, when that possibility has been eliminated, does he accept the true cause. And characters become increasingly involved with drugs, again best illustrated by <u>Thinner</u>'s Dr. Houston. Both elements emphasize the sense of characters out of control. Cancer strikes without warning, an unseen time-bomb "no larger than a good sized walnut" (<u>Roadwork</u> 271). Drugs insidiously distort perceptions of reality, further isolating characters from external reality.

Thus far, I have said little that could not apply to virtually any of King's fictions. The Bachman novels stand alone, however, in that they develop these images, define these themes, detail these motifs without concentrating on horror. Except for <u>Thinner</u>, each seems more science fictional or mainstream than we have come to expect in King. The novels contain images of horror, of course. In <u>The Long Walk</u>, one of the Walkers is described as a "walking haunted house"; he shambles, he stinks, his flesh seems gray, dead. All are characteristics familiar in King's prose, but here they work imagistically. Olson is not haunted in the same sense that The Overlook Hotel is in <u>The Shining</u>. In the context of the novel, the descriptions assert an image of horror, but do not attempt to create the visceral response associated with horror. In spite of the description, Olson remains solidly a "real" character, a boy walking himself to death in a future society not too distant or too different from our own. He is not supernatural, not a shadow where there is no light.

This final characteristic is what fully differentiates the earlier Bachman novels from King's other works. They are insistently non-horrific; what horror they evoke is of a radically different order than vampires or ghosts or malevolent, sentient Plymouth Furies can create. More like <u>Cujo</u> than <u>The Shining</u>, they assert the actuality of horror within the commonplace.

CHAPTER III

RAGE

In the Spring, 1982 <u>Sourcebook</u>, Stephen King published an article called "My High School Horrors," defining six horrors he had experienced as a high-school teacher: The Thing That Wouldn't Shut Up, The Classroom Of The Living Dead, The Smell From Hell, The Incredible Osculating Creature, The Horror Of The Unknown Noises, and The Monster That Wouldn't Turn Off Its Radio. While King's treatment is humorous, the subject is not. In an interview published with the article, King identified what he considered the greatest horror facing high school students:

> Not being able to interact, to get along and establish lines of communication. It's the fear I had, the fear of not being able to make friends, the fear of being afraid and not being able to tell anyone you're afraid. The feelings of inadequacy and of not having anybody to turn to--a teacher, a counselor, a girlfiend, a boyfriend, the guy at the next locker--and say, "I'm afraid I can't make it on this level," whether you mean getting a date for the prom or passing Algebra II. There's a constant fear that <u>I am alone</u>. Mentally, you feel you're running a fever. That's when people need a close relationship, especially outside the family. Inside the family things are often very tense: people say little more than "Please pass the butter" or "Give me the rolls." And all the time kids are deathly afraid that they won't be able to get along. (Bellows 33)

This statement provides insight into King's early fiction, particularly a number of short stories. His experiences in school reflect through stories such as "Cain Rose Up" (1968), "Here There Be Tygers" (1968), and "Strawberry Spring" (1968). After teaching high-school English from 1971-1973, his perspectives shifted slightly, resulting in Carrie (1974) and stories such as "Suffer the Little Children " (1972), in which Miss Sidley destroys the little monsters in her class; and "Sometimes They Come Back" (1974), with Jim Norman as both instructor and, through his nightmares and nightmares come to life, student.

Perhaps more importantly, however, these stories lay groundwork for the final versions of Rage and The Long Walk, archetypal fictions of adolescent behavior and growth, but without the supernatural elements of Carrie. After all, King argues, there is horror enough in being young without having to create more.

"Here There Be Tygers," for example, is not only evocative in its own right, but also seems an early sketch of the early chapters of Rage, modified to incorporate the horror that had already become King's trademark. In each story, a student named Charles, frustrated by his teacher, leaves class and goes to the bathroom, where he confronts a creature, either external or internal. Both stories climax with the boy killing his teacher, the first through inaction, the second through action. There are, of course, differences between the stories, the most significant being the nature of the tiger in "Here There Be Tygers," but the plot outlines seem strikingly similar.

"Cain Rose Up" and "Strawberry Spring" likewise suggest King's concerns in Rage. While the first may be more directly relevant to Roadwork, especially in its treatment of slowly developing anger, both also suggest depths of frustration and unspoken (and unspeakable) anger beneath tranquil surfaces. In both, students resort to the only available outlet: violence. Rage examines this outlet in greater detail.

The most intriguing similarities, however, occur between Carrie, King's first published novel, and Rage, the first of the Bachman novels. In each, the central characters are high school students at odds with themselves, with their families, and with their fellow students. Both novels define isolation and fear, frustration and disappointment, and (most critically) rage--an undefinable, destructive rage that spreads inward and outward and can be assuaged only by an explosion. In Carrie, the outburst constitutes the climax of the novel; in Rage, it occurs within the first few chapters, and the remaining narrative explains, defines, and in part resolves it.

Even on a first reading, there are a number of other similarities between Rage and Carrie, however. If Carrie were to focus more directly on the school, shifting Carrie from adolescent girl first experiencing puberty to adolescent male undergoing similar tensions, one summary could serve equally well for both. Both were written early in King's career; both confront the internal pressures of high-school society; both illustrate the destruction implicit in fragmented, distorted families; both pit a single individual, helpless to understand his or her own motives and identity, against concentric circles of social pressure. Both detail growth and maturity in characters, primarily secondary characters in the school. Both begin in implicit violence, heavily sexual in implication, and end in destruction, Carrie in physical destruction, Rage in psychological destruction. Both describe an individual ostracized by family and peers, trapped in the maze of guilt and misunderstanding that often characterizes King's visions of high school. Both protagonists are children who can no longer act as children but do not yet know how to act as adults. Given the portrayals of the adult world in each novel, perhaps they do not want to know how.

Rage is more than just an early movement toward Carrie, however. It represents one of King's earliest attempts at the novel form itself. Although Joan Smith refers to The Long Walk as King's "oldest full novel . . . done while he was a freshman at the University of Maine in Orono" (1), she mentions Rage as having been written during King's senior year in high school. Castle Rock: The Stephen King Newsletter is more precise: the first forty pages of Rage were written while King was in high school, and The Long Walk was written while King was in college (#3, 9). If not his first completed novel, then, Rage was an early attempt at a novel-length production. The text indicates, however, that King revised his original versions of Rage between 1973 and its publication in 1977: he refers to film versions of Jaws (1973; pp. 4, 192) and The Exorcist (1975; p. 41), showing that he re-worked at least those passages. A reference to John Travolta (91) could suggest the film version of Carrie (1976). As a result, readers expecting to see "early" King may be disappointed; as it stands, Rage seems contemporary with Carrie.

It parallels Carrie as well in being adolescent in subject and tone, as is The Long Walk. In this sense, Rage does reflect an early King; it explores the pressures of young people in high school, suggesting throughout empathy for the young.

It is very much a novel of adolescent rebellion, including an allusion to James Dean, the archetypal teen-age rebel (70). Even more significantly, there are no sympathetic characters over thirty in the novel; both of Charlie Decker's victims are thirty-seven. Adolescents form the nucleus of virtually every relationship examined in Rage.

King presents parents, for example, from the child's perspective, at that difficult stage when parents cease being perfect and become undeniably human, although for Charlie Decker, that revelation had taken place years before. The novel concerns itself more with Charlie working out his own responses to his father and mother. For others, the moment of revelation occurs during the novel, as characters open up in front of their classmates and reveal painful things about themselves, their parents, and their relationships. Grace Stanner and Irma Bates fight verbally and physically, Grace defending her mother against Irma's accusations. Yet the fight ends with

Grace's admission, "My mother fucks . . . and I love her" (98), a moment of public and private acceptance resulting in an outburst of applause from the students. Flaws in parents are examined, itemized, then accepted as inevitable in an adult world.

King also examines relationships between students and adults in authority over them. His conclusions are straightforward and devastating. Neither principals, teachers, nor psychological counselors prove adequate to their positions. They insist on seeing Charlie at best as a child and at worst as an abstraction. Given their functions within the social structure, they are more concerned with socialization than with humanity.

Finally, <u>Rage</u> focuses on relationships among high school students, primarily sexual relationships, although Charlie's friendship with Joe McKennedy becomes important in the final chapters. Their love and hate, jealousy and envy, even their ignorance of and indifference to how others feel, become central as others join Charlie in speaking out. Friendships are made and broken during the four hours Charlie holds his class hostage. Sanity itself becomes suspect as the line between truth and illusion, surface appearance and underlying reality, first blurs then grows startlingly clear. Such revelation is reserved only for the young, however; adults may be stripped of their pretensions, forced momentarily to play Charlie's game, but there is no evidence that any of them change. <u>Rage</u> is about and for adolescents struggling to enter the adult world. The struggle is painful but necessary. King externalizes what most adolescents experience internally.

At its simplest level, <u>Rage</u> deals with anger. It defines the fragmentation of social forms and institutions intended to channel anger and aggression. In the novel, those channels cease to function, either gradually over the course of years, or suddenly, as Charlie Decker's actions force the adults and children involved to assess their own actions. Anger, Charlie discovers, is a "very difficult emotion for a programmed adolescent to handle" (139); most of the characters must resolve their own unspoken rage directed towards themselves, their parents, their friends. Charlie provides the impetus, expressing his anger by shooting Mrs. Underwood and Mr. Vance. Later, he realizes that his own expression is inadequate. Rather than killing Mrs. Underwood, he should have shot Ted Jones; the body at his feet is a "classic case of misplaced aggression" (190).

In <u>Carrie</u>, rage remains largely internalized. Few of the characters find outlets for their fears and frustrations, except sublimated (and occasionally explicit) violence. Stella Horan describes Margaret White's response to seeing her in a brief swimming suit as "Rage. Complete insane rage . . . . Her face was all scrunched up, and it was a gargoyle's face" (25). The choice of gargoyle as image seems appropriate, both for <u>Carrie</u> and for <u>Rage</u>. The pent-up emotions can be expressed only in images of horror: Carrie wandering the streets of Chamberlain, blindly destroying everything in her path, as mindless as the rage that consumes her; or Charlie Decker shooting Mrs. Underwood, not for anything she had done, but because of his frustrations with Tom Denver, Don Grace, Carl Decker, and every other adult in his world. In <u>Carrie</u>, King represents the anger by means of horror; in <u>Rage</u>, he uses extreme extensions of everyday experience. Horror occurs only as image, not as actuality.

The anger results from a generic disintegration of institutions--home, family, school, society. As is common in King's fiction, <u>Rage</u> contains virtually no identifiably healthy family unit. Decker's family lies at the center of the novel. Carl Decker is the "Friendly Neighborhood Creaking Thing" (190), a reference to the violent love-making Charlie hears at night. He is the monster who throws his four-year-old son to the ground for breaking storm windows and lies about it to his wife. He is the man who threatens to slit his wife's nose if she is unfaithful, not caring that his nine-year-old son is listening. He is the man who threatens to kill his teenage son with a garden rake, deferring only when Charlie reciprocates with a hatchet. He is the man who has hated Charlie for as long as the boy can remember.

Mothers are little better. Charlie is an only child; his mother never really wanted another. As such, he is over-protected as well as neglected. Throughout Rage, mothers seem uniquely incapable of understanding children's needs, just as Margaret White seems intent upon destroying Carrie when Carrie ceases to act according to Margaret's needs; Carrie is irrelevant until her power forces Margaret to acknowledge her. Even then, the mother's immediate response is not to help Carrie, but to kill her. Mothers in Rage do not externalize their selfishness quite so extremely, but the underlying pattern is there. Charlie's mother forces him to attend a birthday party dressed in a corduroy suit, complete with bow tie, even though everyone else wears jeans and T-shirts. She cares nothing for Charlie's embarrassment; her only concern, he discovers years later, was that he make the right impression on Carol Granger's mother. In the same chapter, Charlie recounts his mother's reaction to a picture puzzle, "Last Berry in the Patch," given her as a joke and a challenge by Carl Decker one Christmas. She worked on it for three days, ignoring husband and son, completed the puzzle, then put it in the attic for good. She had made her point.

Other mothers are, in their own ways, equally monstrous. Mrs. Dano, Pig Pen's mother, cares less for her children than for her gossip. Carol Granger's mother epitomizes King's attitudes toward mothers in Rage: "She was every Japanese horror monster ever made, all rolled into one, Ghidra, Mothra, Godzilla, Rodan, and Tukkan the Terrible trundling across the Granger living room" (122). In pysical description and psychological makeup, she nearly doubles for the title character in King's chilling story "Gramma" or Mrs. Leighton in "The Blue Air Compressor." Charlie Decker represents in extremis the situation of every other person in the room: he must stand without support from the two people society defines as responsible for a child's welfare. Throughout the novel, Charlie refers to childhood trauma, to parental neglect or abuse as excuses for anti-social behavior. He ridicules the idea, yet underneath the ridicule lies the nagging suspicion that there is truth in it.

If parents fail individually, schools fail collectively and miserably. Parents should love their children; there is, however, no law requiring principals to love students. In <u>Rage</u> the adults specifically responsible for educating children collapse when confronted with Charlie Decker, a student who refuses to accept the platitudes of education, what he refers to as the "splendid sticky web of Mother Education" (7). At every level within the school, adults fail themselves as well as their students.

Teachers appear only briefly in the novel. Charlie shoots two and attacks one with a wrench; a fourth retreats when Charlie fires into the door jamb. The only two fatalities in the novel are teachers responsible for subjects in which Charlie is least integrated. Mrs. Jean Underwood (a paradoxically sylvan, non-threatening name; one is reminded of Tolkien´s Underhill) teaches algebra. She demonstrates control, rationality, precision of thought and action . . . traits Charlie has never developed. His irrationality forms the basis for the novel; he boasts that the principal was prepared for anything except irrationality. For Decker, the universe itself is irrational, blending Jekyll and Hyde, light and dark, sanity and insanity (33). His lack of control forces him to assert an artificial control within the classroom. For the first time, he boasts, the adults must play <u>his</u> game. But by the end of the novel, as layers of self-deception peel away, he even loses control of his own game. In the final chapter, he deceives the hospital staff into thinking he likes custard; he has a secret again, he boasts, and has regained a degree of control.

The second victim, Mr. Vance, is a history teacher. Charlie Decker and his peers have little sense of history, tradition, and heritage. Their lives are controlled by passion, by hatred and sex and frustration. The process which should help them adjust and become part of the historical continuum of civilization and society fails; Charlie sees the girls turning into mindless suburban housewives, unthinking and uncaring (an image King included in his "Garbage Truck" column on May 8, 1969). For them, history and all that it suggests are dead.

It also seems important, in terms of comparison with Carrie, that the teachers in Rage remain ineffective. None develops as a character. Mrs. Underwood and Mr. Vance play passive roles as victims; Mr. Carlson pressures Charlie into striking him with a pipe wrench; Mr. Johnson is a near victim. Otherwise, we see no interaction between teachers and students. In Carrie, there is at least minimal hope as Rita Desjardin attempts to reach Carrie. Her attempt misfires, supplying too little encouragement too late, but she does try. Unlike adults in Rage, she takes responsibility for her actions; in the aftermath of Carrie's devastating revenge, she resigns: "I feel I would kill myself before ever teaching again. Late at night I keep thinking: If I had only reached out to that girl, if only, if only . . . " 197). At least she tried; in Rage, no one even goes that far.

If teachers are passive victims, advisors are incompetents. Don Grace is pretentious and self-deluded, distanced from the students he should help. Charlie turns the game on Grace, forcing the psychiatrist to reveal his own motives, sexual practices, hopes, and frustrations. Charlie tries to break him, threatening to shoot a hostage if Grace leaves the intercom without permission. Grace argues that he cannot take the responsibility. "My God, you've been taking the responsibility ever since they let you loose from college" (81), Charlie screams; now that Grace has an opportunity to be truly responsible for life or death, he backs away.

This interchange begins King's critique of contemporary psychology, already implied in Decker's attitudes toward parents and parental guilt. "I won't play a cheap parlor game with human lives for party favors," Grace says; that,

Charlie replies, defines contemporary psychiatry perfectly: playing games with people's minds. Grace is willing to penetrate Charlie's mind and exhibit what he finds there. He is less willing to be penetrated. Charlie probes Grace's sexuality to reveal the psychiatrist's own psychological state. Grace tries to bring Charlie into line with the rules of the adults' game. His first comment over the intercom, spoken in a voice radiating calmness and certainty, is horribly inappropriate for the context: "Now, you've committed a pretty anti-social act, wouldn't you agree?" (77) His expertise is equally inappropriate, since he also cannot respond rationally to irrationality. By the end of the conversation, Grace is destroyed psychologically, a state reflected in his physical stance as he walks like an old man from the building. King explicitly denies the promise in the psychiatrist's name; Grace and his kind cannot help Charlie, since they are already victims of their own delusions.

The highest educational authority in the novel, the principal, represents the greatest failure within the system. Even the principal's office suggests Thomas Denver's inability to understand students. The outer office is cluttered, with a slatted gate and a safe set into the wall. Miss Marble, his secretary, is imagistically as coldly distanced as Denver is . . . or tries to be.

Denver sounds like a character in a horror film, cadaverous, reminiscent of John Carradine. Denver believes that he is in the "kid business," yet admits that he cannot understand Charlie and others like him, in spite of his pretensions to sincerity and concern. Nor can he respond other than through undisguised anger (rage, to borrow the novel's title) when Charlie answers him with irrationality and contempt. Charlie throws Denver's boast about progressive education back in his face, then attacks with obscenity and sexual innuendo. When Denver chases him from the room, Charlie bursts into Miss Marble's office, his shirt-tails out and fly unzipped, screaming that Denver had tried to rape him . . . certainly not the last image of rape in the novel.

The central authority figure emerges as "furious, silly, and guilty" (23), incapable of controlling the discussion, Charlie, or even himself. Yet he is the person entrusted with educating and socializing students.

His role in <u>Rage</u> contrasts sharply with the principal's in <u>Carrie</u>. Charlie's tragedy occurs because authority betrays him; Carrie's occurs in spite of attempts to help her. In both cases, for opposite reasons, each principal unknowingly initiates the major crisis.

Henry Grayle seems open to Carrie's problems. The assistant principal, Mr. Morton, virtually ignores Carrie, even when she sits in the room with him. He assumes that she has had an accident and searches for the proper forms, without consulting her or Rita Desjardin. Desjardin must remind him of Carrie's name; three paragraphs later, he mispronounces her last name, then twice calls her "Cassie" (13-14). "That's not my name," Carrie screams, but she is a cipher to him. Within half a page, he misses her name again, substituting Wright for White. Like Charlie Decker for Tom Denver, Carrie simply does not exist as an individual for Morton; she is merely an extension of his function in the school. After Carrie leaves his office, he brushes away ashes spilled from an overturned ashtray, unconsciously symbolizing the movement of <u>Carrie</u>: when Carrie makes herself noticeable, the survivors can only clean up the ashes.

Principal Grayle, on the other hand, promises hope. He does not confront Carrie directly; perhaps that suggests why, in spite of his efforts, he fails to support Carrie. Instead, Grayle meets with John Hargenson, the father of Carrie's chief antagonist. Hargenson is impressively controlled: the school must allow Chris to attend the Prom and allow Desjardin's contract to lapse at the end of the shool year. Grayle counterattacks, vigorously defending Carrie, showing an understanding of his students and their problems that lies beyond Tom Denver's ability. He threatens to counter-sue and forces Hargenson to back down. On the surface, he has protected Carrie, fulfilling his responsibility as educator and administrator.

The irony, of course, is that by standing up for Carrie he dooms her. By confirming the sanctions against Chris Hargenson, he makes the bloody Prom Night virtually inevitable, yet only later can he understand the implications of his decision. By indirectly helping Carrie discover herself, he contributes to her death. In spite of his positive representation in <u>Carrie</u>, the principal functions as a catalyst for destruction. On the surface Grayle and Denver differ, but King implies that they share deeper meanings, in effect if not in motivation.

In his characterization of educators and advisors, King almost forces an inverted (or perhaps better, perverted) theological reading of two names, <u>Grace</u> and <u>Grayle</u>, words associated with humanity's search for identity and understanding. The first is an abstract; the second, in an alternate spelling, a literary image for the first. Yet in neither book can the names fulfil their promise. Don "God-Give-Us-Grace" and Henry Grayle foster destruction, not salvation; Carrie's quest, like Charlie's, must inevitably fail.

The two names also define larger circles of failures within society itself, exemplified by religion and education in <u>Carrie</u>, by education in <u>Rage</u> (although Irma Bates' moralistic diatribe invites the reader to test religion as assiduously as any other vehicle for socialization). For Charlie Decker, the process becomes a game called "Are you ready for tomorrow's society?" The purpose of the game is to introduce adolescents into the adult world. The rules establish roles for adult and child alike, but the adults have broken the rules. They do not meet their responsibilities, leaving the children to work out things for themselves, to extricate themselves from what Charlie calls a "mass puberty cramp" (123). Sexuality absorbs the students, as do relationships: parent to child, society to child, child to child. Ideally society should link the levels, but in <u>Rage</u>, links seem entirely missing. Only the last remains to any degree intact.

The relationship of child to child forms the nucleus of the novel. In a sense, everything else is peripheral. Charlie Decker's problems with his mother and father impel him to action; the focus of his action, however, quickly shifts from himself to the others in the classroom. In effect, King works with two narratives. The first entails Charlie's memories of himself and his family; the second and more critical, intertwines with the first and explains it, giving it meaning by defining Charlie's effect on others. By the final chapters of <u>Rage</u>, Charlie no longer controls the game, or is even essential to it. It has infected everyone in the room. Through their self-revelations, characters force deeper understandings of themselves, leading the others along.

In the beginning, Charlie's reminiscences interrupt the present-time narrative. Chapters 5, 14, and 16 re-create his past, first as he thinks to himself, then as he talks to the class as part of "getting it on." These flashbacks provide important information for the reader, particularly since the novel is told with Charlie as first-person narrator. The reader cannot otherwise uncover the past. Later, other students reveal their secrets as well, initiating a process Charlie himself does not fully understand.

Although there are small excursions into background throughout the early chapters, Chapter 20 signals a new thrust to the novel. Before, Charlie was central; narrative chapters outlined his actions and the reactions of others to him, while flashbacks concentrated on his relationships. Other students occasionally intruded into Charlie's game plan, but he was securely in control. In Chapter 20, however, Grace Stanner and Irma Bates confront each other in the first full-scale external conflict within the class.

Grace Stanner, whose name recalls the Blue Ribbon Laundry foreman in King's "The Mangler" and whose mother works in a laundry (suggesting a connection between King and Bachman; Margaret White also works in a Blue Ribbon Laundry), encourages Charlie after his confrontation with Don Grace. She shocks and surprises many of the students, but Charlie feels less surprise; after all, he says, there are others besides himself who want to see heads roll.

What does surprise him, however, is Irma Bates' violent reaction to Grace and to everything Charlie has said and done. Irma opposes Grace Stanner in every respect. Grace is small, petite, pretty in a rather suggestive way; she shows her tight sweaters and short skirts off to every advantage, while Irma Bates, on the other hand, reflects what Carrieta White might have become. She is large, slow, unattractive, with a poor complexion and batrachian features, epitomizing what King referred to as "The Smell From Hell" in "My High School Horrors" (32). Her name, of course, suggests Norman Bates of Psycho, an allusion supported by King's later reference in Rage to Bates' mother (170). More critically, she views everything and everyone from a narrow, fundamentalist morality and is deeply disturbed by what she has seen. She responds to disruptions in her orderly universe by attacking Grace's mother in terms that vividly recall Margaret White's distorted attitudes toward sexuality in Carrie, calling Grace a "whore's daughter" and a "slut's daughter."

At this point, Charlie steps in. Grace is surprised, but Irma seems relieved and vindicated, as if Charlie were a "justly intervening god" (92), and uses the sudden stasis to resume her attack on Grace's mother's reputation. King makes it clear, however, that Irma's apparent courage allies with terror as she attempts to define events within the framework of her stifling religious background.

Charlie does not intervene to defend Irma, however, but to orchestrate the conflict. He establishes a context for the girls' pent-up hostilities. Like the schoolboys in William Golding's Lord of the Flies, he speaks of the need for structures that allow civilized resolution of individual differences. He draws a circle on the floor; the girls enter the circle, knowing that to step outside until the matter has been resolved means death. He creates a figurative pentagram, imprisoning the girls with the monsters that live inside them. Within the circle, the girls must control their need for violent reaction and follow a complex code of behavior. Charlie's game allows each to attack and to defend, physically and verbally. The class watches, entranced; only Ted Jones objects. "They were watching," Charlie says about the others in the room, "and maybe what they saw was a little bit of their own souls, flashed at them in a cracked mirror" (96).

The conflict ends abruptly. Irma blurts out an apology and collapses in tears, accepting for the first time who and what she is, just as Grace defiantly accepts her mother for what *she* is and does. The class applauds Grace's courage, but the matter is not yet settled. As Irma stands and repeats her apology, Grace fulfills the promise of her name, a promise explicitly denied in the preceding chapter by Don Grace. Grace accepts the apology and forgives Irma, which leads to a second, deeper level of self-revelation for Irma. She admits her loneliness and isolation, accepting everything Grace said about her as true. Her admission is as painful as Grace's and elicits a similar response; three other girls sit down with her, presumably to teach her how to care for herself and make herself more attractive.

By the end of the chapter, Grace and Irma have reached new plateaus of individual understanding about themselves, their sexuality, and their relationships with others. Their achievement required physical and mental pain, yet like the frantic struggles of a chrysalis to escape its cocoon, that pain leads to something greater. By throwing off the protective layerings imposed by adults, the girls can define their own identity. Charlie has accomplished more in the forty-five minutes since he shot Mrs. Underwood than all of the Don Graces had accomplished in years.

From this point, the novel concentrates on the other students; control slips from Charlie as individuals speak out, publicly working through their private frustrations. In Chapter 21, "Pig Pen" Dano erupts with a diatribe aginst his mother's naivete, insensitivity, and cruelty. The epitome of pragmatic adulthood, she drowns kittens and sells her son's car to send her pregnant daughter away. She is too stupid to realize that everyone, including her own son, sees through her delusions about herself. Pig Pen finally says simply that if he had more "stick," he would kill his mother himself.

Two chapters later, Carol Granger takes the floor, promising to tell about her sex life if Charlie will tell about his. She explains what it is like as a girl suddenly aware of sexuality and of the dirtiness associated with it in contemporary society, the depersonalization of women into things that parallels the failure of education, with its depersonalization of students into things: "And that's like being bright, too. They want to stuff things into your head until it's all filled up. It's a different hole, that's all. That's all" (141).

Her self-revelation concludes when she says bluntly that Ted Jones had made love to her and that it wasn't all that great. Charlie loses contact with his own definition of reality, raises his pistol to kill Ted . . . and is shot.

The bullet, fired by a marksman from outside, strikes a padlock in Charlie's pocket, throwing him to the ground without injuring him. He regains control by threatening again to kill Ted Jones. And the students' narratives continue.

The next story involves Ted Jones even more directly. His girlfriend, Susan Cross, takes the stand against him, exposing not only her fears and needs, but his as well.

Susan Cross is one of two characters who connect Rage with The Stand (1978). Jean Underwood shares surnames with Larry Underwood, one of The Stand's protagonists; other than the connection by name (a clue to "Bachman's" identity, on a par with the reference to "John Swithen" in Carrie [122]), there seems little relationship between the characters. Susan Cross, on the other hand, not only shares surnames with Nadine Cross, but fills a similarly pivotal position in the narrative.

Nadine Cross is critical in The Stand. She

"crosses" over to support the Walking Dude and oppose Mother Abagail, an action inversely symbolized as her hair turns from black to white. Her action is important since she supports Harold Lauder's betrayal and becomes an essential part of the Dark Man's plans. She acts paradoxically, however, as her rejection of the Dark Man and death at his hands initiate the disintegration of his forces.

Susan Cross's indictments of Ted Jones focus attention on him as central character--as the core of the novel. To borrow Carol Granger's metaphor, he is an apple that looks good on the outside, but is wormy inside. Initially, Susan angers Ted by talking about their making love. Ted reacts first by glowering at Charlie; then by blanking all expression from his face; then by curling his lips, imagistically reducing himself to a dog; and finally, as Susan refers to the sex act itself, by blushing.

But Susan is not finished. Ted's lovemaking leaves her feeling empty, unreal, like a painted backdrop for a stage play. To define her identity and her "reality," she returns to the Rollerdrome where she and Ted dated and picks up a greasy, smelly boy. As she recounts their violent, abrupt, loveless coupling, Ted finally reacts, first with horror and revulsion, then with an explosive outburst that sounds like nothing so much as Irma Bates' or Margaret White's hypersensitive sense of sin. At that moment, the narrative irrevocably shifts toward its primary target.

As noted earlier, there are two stories in _Rage_: the direct narrative of Charlie Decker and his actions in the school, and the indirect narrative developed through flashbacks. While that structure is basic to the novel, it is also misleading.

In a critical sense, _Rage_ is not so much about Charlie Decker as it is about Ted Jones, even though Jones speaks only rarely and never as much as other students. Instead, he represents the standard against which they are all measured. To that extent he may in fact be the central character, in spite of (and perhaps because of) Charlie's presence as narrator. Charlie does not change substantially in Rage. He serves as a catalyst for others, a means of externalizing their anger and frustration. The changes in Ted Jones, on the other hand, epitomize the flaws King defines throughout the novel, as Decker strips the veneers of adult accommodation from Jones.

From the beginning, Ted Jones opposes Charlie Decker. They represent different social levels. Ted is a mover and a doer. He wears the right clothes, drives the right car. His parents belong to the right circles. In everything, Ted is what Charlie is not.

Ted also balances Charlie in the classroom. He is the only one who moves after Charlie kills Vance and fires at Johnson. He gets up and locks the door, thereby paradoxically protecting the adults and potentially condemning himself and the other students to injury or death. Ted maneuvers to shift control from Charlie to himself, and from there to the adults outside. When another student, George Yannick, reminds Charlie that the intercom is still on and that anyone in the principal's office can hear everything said in the class, Charlie switches the intercom off; Ted calls Yannick a "bigmouth son of a bitch" (50). When Charlie ridicules Ted's mother's alcoholism, the class is fascinated by Ted's discomfort; again, he takes center place.

By the mid-point of Rage, King has established the parameters of confrontation: Charlie Decker's obvious insanity against Ted Jones' apparent sanity. The two key words, of course, are "obvious" and "apparent"; Charlie's manipulation of the students does more than help them individually to discover their own identities. It also helps them penetrate the deception that Ted Jones represents.

The initial discovery that Ted quit the football team because of his mother's alcoholism wounds Ted deeply, but is only a taste of what is to come. Increasingly, Charlie uses Ted as the primary target of his frustration. He notes explicitly that he should not have shot Jean

Underwood; he should have shot Ted. And he begins to understand that Ted represents attitudes that Charlie cannot accommodate. Ted is to the other students, Charlie decides, what Eisenhower was to the "dedicated liberals" in the fifties: "You had to like him, that style, that grin, that record, those good intentions, but there was something exasperating and a tiny bit slimy about him" (109). Charlie admits that he is obsessed by Ted; as the exercises in self-revelation continue, they point more and more at Ted Jones, culminating in Sandra Cross´ implicit indictment of Ted´s moral and ethical code, coupled with her explicit condemnation of him as lover. To seek "reality," she resorts to an obnoxious, possibly dangerous stranger.

By that point, Charlie understands one thing: the only hostage in the classroom is Ted Jones (151). Irma Bates, in fact, leaves to go to the bathroom and returns of her own volition. Twenty pages later, the shift in emphasis is complete. Charlie has the "crazy feeling" that the class is holding <u>him</u>, rather than the other way around; and that all of them are, in turn, holding Ted hostage (173).

In a surprising move, Charlie announces at noon that he will release the students and surrender at 1:00, provided that the police do not attempt any SWAT-team tactics and that they allow him to pull the shades. Charlie uses the first half-hour to narrate his final brutal encounter with his father´s hatred, then turns to the class and asks how many understand what the final order of business for the day must be.

Every hand raises . . . except Ted Jones´. Carol finally puts their determination into words: "We have to help show Ted where he has gone wrong" (194). One by one, they attack, first verbally, then physically. They bear witness against him, with Charlie as judge and prosecutor. The others order Ted to shut up. They accuse him of trying to be superior, of being a "soul killer," of hiding his own flawed character, of abusing trust, of masturbating (which makes him angrier than anything else).

Ted threatens to walk out, challenging Charlie to shoot him. Instead, the others stop him. In a scene frighteningly reminiscent of Simon's death in Golding's <u>The Lord of the Flies</u> (the killing there takes place at the foot of Castle Rock), the students engulf Ted Jones, hitting, kicking; they stamp on his foot and break bones; they pour ink over his head, degrading and breaking him. To paraphrase Shirley Jackson's "The Lottery," Ted Jones screamed, and then they were upon him. Charlie himself does not move.

At one o'clock the students leave, except for Charlie Decker and Ted Jones. In a sense, the novel has finished. Charlie is in some oddly appropriate way sane, by his own standards if not by society's. Ted Jones, the epitome of childhood adaptation to maturity, is insane. He had come to stand for the illusions foisted on children by parents, by school, and by society as a whole. In order to shatter their individual illusions and delusions, the students had to shatter him as well.

The final four chapters move away from the primary setting and action of <u>Rage</u>, much as King withdrew from the settings of <u>Carrie</u> in the brief "Part Three: Wreckage" in that novel. Chapter 32 is a one-page document declaring Charles Everett Decker guilty of murdering Jean Alice Underwood and John Downes Vance (identified by a radio broadcast in Chapter 21 as Patrick Vance, an unexplained contradiction). Decker, being legally insane, is to be remanded to the state institution in Augusta. Characteristically, Charlie adds his own pithy interpretation of the legal jargon.

Chapter 33, also about one page long, is a memo dated November 3, 1976, over two months after the incident at Placerville High School, indicating that Theodore Jones remains catatonic and that his condition is in fact deteriorating.

Chapter 34, the longest of the four, is a two-and-a-half page letter dated December 5, 1976, from Joe McKennedy to Charlie. Although Joe never appears in the novel, he is important as Charlie's best and perhaps only friend. He serves as a foil to Charlie Decker, foreshadowing the relationship between Dennis Guilder and Arnie Cunningham in *Christine*. Joe, like Dennis, is popular and athletic, making friends easily. Charlie, like Arnie, is a loner, the odd man out--in his own terms, a fifth wheel. He is at best tolerated, but only because of his relationship to Joe. He admits that he very nearly worships Joe (120).

Hearing from Joe, then, should suggest to Charlie what effect he has had on the others. And it does. The letter relays bits of local news about Sandra Cross, Pig Pen and Dick Keene (a passage censored by the hospital staff): a paragraph on Carol Granger's valedictory speech, "Self-Integrity and a Normal Response to It," which had appeared in *Seventeen* magazine. Irma Bates, now dating, is a political activist. Grace Stanner is engaged. On the surface, the letter is innocuous, but given the self-revelations that led to each of those situations, it is at best ironic. In spite of what they discovered about themselves, and in spite of what they witnessed in the classroom, most of the students have become Ted Joneses. Joe is himself studying diligently at Boston University, reading James Cain and considering becoming an English major--a far cry from the Joe McKennedy of Chapter 1 who reveled in giving "some bag" a hard time about building a memorial at the school to honor students killed in wartime; or the Joe McKennedy of Chapter 8 who paraded through the school halls with a Con-Tact strip plastered on his forehead. Irma Bates has broken out of her self-imposed isolation; there may be hope for her. But otherwise, the Ted Joneses are ahead.

The final chapter is the shortest: four brief paragraphs. Charlie is alone, completely isolated within himself. It is time to turn off the light, he says. "Good night."

Since *Rage* succeeds or fails on the strength of its characters, to examine them closely is perhaps the best way to discuss the novel. The novel is virtually without plot: Charlie Decker kills two teachers and holds a class of students hostage. They talk, someone shoots at Charlie, the students talk some more, one student gets beaten up, and then Charlie lets them go. He is wounded and sent to an asylum.

The bare outline does not suggest the complexity of the book, however. <u>Rage</u> is less the story of a single individual than a chronicle of shifting relationships, loyalties, hatreds. Its "action" lies in dialogue and narrative; physical action is at times peripheral, almost irrelevant.

Yet King uses the stasis of the novel to great effect. Through it, he is able to examine a number of issues important to himself and his audience. He scathingly criticizes the process by which children become adults, and thereby criticizes adult society itself. The children not only are not given adequate guidance through the morass of adolescence, but should they emerge on the other side, they find nothing worth the struggle. Adolescent rebellion becomes a hollow show; in spite of Charlie's actions, little changes for the students.

In addition, King explores several themes that recur throughout his works. <u>Rage</u> is as much about sexuality as it is "about" anything, but this is a sexuality devoid of love or caring. Relationships throughout the novel are superficial, physical manifestations of lust, beginning with Carl Decker's performances as the "Creaking Thing," and culminating in Susan Cross' self-prostitution. None of the characters relate any satisfying sexual experiences; and in a sense, sexuality itself becomes a central horror image in the novel. Given Charlie's choice of weapons, it could even be argued that the novel rests on a Freudian, symbolic sublimation of sexuality. As another "Pig Pen" says, "pistols and braces were impotency figures" ("Cain Rose Up"). In addition, as so frequently happens in King's novels, characters are not even sure of their own sexual orientations. Charlie falsely accuses the principal of attempted homosexual rape, which drives Denver to even greater fury than before. Charlie is hypersensitive to Frank Philbrick's voice over the intercom[1]; it reminds him of his father's voice, and suggests homosexuality to him (133); on the next page, Charlie covers for a scatological remark Sylvia makes by referring to his own "certain transsexual tendencies" (134). The central episode of Charlie's narration of his first sexual encounter details his concern for his sexuality; unable to maintain his erection, he wonders whether he might not be "queer" (169).

Compounding these problem is the underlying conflict between sanity and insanity, rationality and irrationality, that colors everything in the novel. If Charlie is insane at the beginning, and Ted sane, the conclusion of Rage becomes highly pessimistic, with Charlie speaking almost as the voice of reason and Ted withdrawn and catatonic. Sanity may be a perilous state; certainly it is a painful one.

This treatment of sanity leads to the foremost strength and the foremost weakness of the novel.

Charlie Decker.

Unlike Carrie, The Shining, or in fact any other King novels (either under his own name or as Richard Bachman), Rage is a first-person narrative. King explores the possibility of first-person narrative only infrequently, and then primarily in his short fiction. Perhaps this is the most telling evidence for Rage as an early work; a central character, isolated from society, self-admittedly caught between sanity and insanity, tells the story directly.

We have no opportunities to enter anyone else's thoughts, which necessitates the narrative structure King chose: flashbacks interspersed with direct narration. It is at times an awkward structure, but necessary to give the novel sufficient depth and breadth of interest. As readers, we feel comfortable seeing through Charlie's perspectives, but only for a limited time. Eventually, King has to show us alternatives, if only to confirm the accuracy of Charlie's perceptions.

This results in two characteristics in Rage. The first, reflecting such stories as Poe's "The Black Cat," reinforces the undercurrent of insanity. Charlie speaks clearly, precisely, rationally. Just as did so many of Poe's murderers, Charlie stands before the reader and asserts his sanity, then details his actions, themselves patently insane, without motivation or justification. It becomes increasingly difficult to empathize with Charlie, at which point King allows control to pass from him to others. We concentrate instead on Ted Jones, remanding Charlie to the background of our own minds, where he speaks simply as narrative voice.

On the other hand, Charlie as narrator gives the novel its most distinctive strength, a vigor and expansiveness of expression that we have come to expect in King. Discussing <u>Rage</u> tends to convert it into a thought-experiment. Opening the text to any page and reading any line reminds us with startling suddenness that in spite of its philosophical or intellectual cargo, it is a novel about <u>people</u>. Charlie Decker speaks with power and authority, in the language of adolescence, with the excitement and strength of adolescence. Whether King was simply speaking for himself and drawing on his own responses to high school, or whether <u>Rage</u> is in fact a revision reflecting a more mature King, is largely irrelevant. What is important is that the novel is compelling. It may be straightforward in structure, simplistic in plot, occasionally clumsy in providing transitions from past to present--but it <u>moves</u>.

Narrower in scope than many of his works, more restricted in time and space (four hours in a single room; except for the flashbacks it parallels the classical unities of tragedy), concentrating more on characterization than external action, and lacking the supernatural horror that has become King's trademark, <u>Rage</u> is nonetheless an impressive novel, and a welcome addition to King's canon.

As the first published "Bachman" novel, <u>Rage</u> must have presented King with a number of problems. He has been asked in interviews about his early, unpublished manuscripts; but by the time many of the interviews were held, he had in fact published at least two of them. Winter's <u>The Art of Darkness</u> refers to King's first attempt at a novel, then to an apparently separate manuscript, "Getting It On," which King completed in 1971 (25). That novel, as King has stated, reminded him of Loren Singer's <u>The Parallax View</u>, so King sent it to Doubleday addressed simply to "The Editor of <u>The Parallax View</u>. Unfortunately, Doubleday decided not to publish the novel.

In a 1981 interview in <u>Starship</u>, Robert Stewart asked King about his early unsold novels. King answered, somewhat hesitantly, that he "did one called . . . trying to go back to the very beginning . . . It's very dusty in that part of my mind. What the hell was the name of that? I cannot remember. Isn't that funny. I've come up totally blank. <u>Getting It On</u>. I did a book called <u>Getting It On</u>" (45-46). By 1981, of course, <u>Getting It On,</u> under its final title <u>Rage</u> had been in print for four years; it would seem that King's inability to remember owed less to time than to a desire to protect the Bachman pseudonym. In this interview, as in others, King remains vague about the early manuscripts[2]; nowhere does he give a precise enough description or plot summary to allow readers to connect them with the Bachman novels.

At last, however, he no longer needs to dissemble. <u>Rage</u> and the others are now clearly where they belong . . . on the shelf with works by Stephen King.

NOTES

[1]King's use of <u>Frank Philbrick</u> as the name of the head of the Maine State Police is surely an ironic reference to Herbert Arthur Philbrick, FBI counter-agent and author of <u>I Led Three Lives</u> (1952). Michelle Slung notes the importance of Philbrick and others associated with the Communist threat of the early fifties for herself and others of King's generation (15).

[2] In a review in <u>The New York Times Book Review</u> dated September 27, 1981, for example, King recounts his first submission to Doubleday, but while he refers to Singer's <u>The Parallax View</u> by name, he avoids any reference to either the name or the content of his own manuscript (McDowell 40).

Chapter IV

THE LONG WALK

If <u>Rage</u> represents King's earliest attempt at the novel form, <u>The Long Walk</u> is his oldest full novel (Smith 1). It is also the Bachman novel for which we have the most background. According to Joan Smith,

> A number of people remembered "The Long Walk" from King's college days, but had been pledged to secrecy. One of King's English professors acknowledged . . . that he knew Richard Bachman as a student at the University of Maine at Orono. The UMO alumni office, however, did not list a Richard Bachman as having ever attended. (2)

It may also be the one Bachman novel, except for <u>Thinner</u>, which provides the clearest external evidence of King's authorship.

In explaining how the mystery of the Bachman novels began to unfold, King stated that he had made several mistakes in the dedications. One novel, he says, was "dedicated to Shawn Littlefield of Hampden, who died." <u>Roadwork</u>, first published in 1981, bears the dedicatory lines:

> In memory of Charlotte Littlefield.
> Proverbs 31:10-28

<u>The Long Walk</u> also bears a dedication to Jim Bishop, Burt Hatlen, and Ted Holmes. Hatlen, increasingly well known as a King scholar, was also King's professor at UMO.

Hatlen's name figures prominently in Winter's discussion of King's early career. In 1966, King attended UMO as a freshman. During that summer, he had begun work on a novel, <u>Getting It On</u> (on

the basis of the title, surely an early draft of
Rage). In his freshman year, however, he completed his first novel, which Winter does not name by title but describes as "a dystopian fantasy set in a parallel world." King submitted the novel to a first-book competition but lost (Art of Darkness 21-22).

During his sophomore year, King showed one of his manuscripts to Hatlen, who read it, recognized King's talent, and supported him in writing and publishing. Since then, Hatlen has emerged as an important critic of King's fictions. In 1982, for example, he published "Beyond the Kittery Bridge: Stephen King's Maine" in Tim Underwood and Chuck Miller's critical anthology Fear Itself: The Horror Fiction of Stephen King. A year later, he published a review-article on Cujo, "The Mad Dog and Maine," in Douglas Winter's Shadowings (1983). And in March of 1984, he read "The Destruction and Re-Creation of the Human Community in Stephen King's The Stand" at a special session of the International Conference on the Fantastic in the Arts devoted to King, who was present as Guest of Honor.[1]

Given Hatlen's connections with King from 1967 to the present, Hatlen's name on the dedication page of a novel published in 1979 could certainly add to the speculation that King wrote The Long Walk.

There is, in addition, one unusual piece of external data that might have linked King with The Long Walk. The first and second printings of The Long Walk are identical, down to a typo on page 240 ("He hopped [sic] he wouldn't hear the shots"), with a single exception. The advertisement page facing the title page of the first edition of The Long Walk lists "More Thrillers from SIGNET": Rage, by Richard Bachman; novels by David Lippincott, James Herbert, and Joseph Gilmore; and, finally, Night Shift, Carrie, The Shining, and 'Salem's Lot, by Stephen King.

In the second printing, the advertisement has been changed to read "SIGNET Titles by Stephen King You'll Want to Read." All references to other authors, including Richard Bachman, have disappeared, replaced by a list of ten King titles; several Herbert titles appear, but in a different listing at the back of the book. It is almost as if Signet were preparing to acknowledge King's authorship.

The Long Walk differs from Rage in a number of ways. Its plot is more streamlined and its characters drawn with a defter hand, less suggestive of stereotype. While its main characters are still adolescents eighteen or under, it is not so much an adolescent novel; it lacks the sense of imminence one finds throughout Rage, as if the author were more mature, more in control of his subject and his craft. It suggests a genre shift for King, since The Long Walk is explicitly set in an alternate America of the near future, making the novel to some degree science fiction. Such a classification is vague at best, given the emphasis on characterization and de-emphasis on technological developments readers might expect in science fiction. But while Rage might happen at any time and any place, even in contemporary American society, The Long Walk could not . . . yet.

It is also a more literary novel, richly allusive without becoming overly so. The characters are for the most part high-school boys. Several are familiar with literature and literary types; one of the Walkers, in fact, plans to write a book about the experience, if he survives.

He does not, but the sense of literature underlying the novel remains strong throughout. Perhaps because several of the boys are intelligent and well-read, King can introduce literary allusions into the text, often subtly, frequently without the reader noticing it, and always to great effect.

Some of the allusions add momentary depth. In a novel obsessed with contemplating death, Peter McVries' paraphrase of "The grave's a fine and quiet place" (45) seems eminently appropriate; the remainder of Marvell's couplet underlies The Long Walk, however, as Ray Garraty and the others confront their own deaths. Several Walkers are self-admitted virgins, not yet fully aware of sexuality. One of the Walkers learns too late that "none . . . do there embrace," as his frantic, rushed attempt at sexual release leads to his death. The Marvell line seems on the surface merely a literary ornament; in a deeper sense, however, it resonates throughout the novel.

Elsewhere in The Long Walk, King refers briefly to the master of horror fiction, Edgar Allan Poe, coupling him with Stephen Foster to create a parody of horror as genre; but again, the imagistic suggestions implicit in a reference to Poe reverberate throughout the narrative. The Long Walk is not a horror novel, but it does depend for its effects upon assertions of horror, a technique common to both Poe and Lovecraft.

King frequently uses the word horror as a touchstone in critical passages, referring tangentially to his more usual genre. In The Long Walk, the episodes are indeed horrific, not through evoking stereotypic horror images, but by suggesting the extremes of suffering the human mind and body can endure. Olson's death is a particularly graphic example. It begins with Garraty's description of him; the boy "shambles," seems more a haunted house than a living being. He "had fouled himself"; he "smelled bad" (154). He seems more ghoul or zombie than human, more at home in Creepshow than in science fiction.

A few pages later, Olson attacks the Squads guarding the Walkers. As punishment, they gut-shoot him. King vividly describes Olson as he struggles to walk, viscera spilling through the boy's fingers. Garraty reacts with "wonder and horror," nauseated but compelled to watch, thereby compelling the reader to watch as well. When the horror is complete and Olson dead, Garraty can say nothing but "It's not fair!" Elsewhere, the Walkers are compared to concentration camp horrors (201) who pass a textile mill rearing "turrets into the fog like a filthy medieval castle" (208). Although when writing as Bachman, King avoids most supernatural horror (except in Thinner), The Long Walk frequently uses language to generate the neurological responses of horror in the reader.

The novel also refers to several contemporary writers. Ray Bradbury appears in a quick reference to one of his short stories, in which the same faces appear in crowds gathered around accident victims (117-118); the Walkers begin to have the same sense about the crowds--the Great God Crowd--that gather along the highway hoping to see a boy get his ticket. Golding's <u>Lord of the Flies</u> is alluded to in a character named Percy, whose death scene recalls Golding's novel. McVries' hysterical vision of flies crawling on the Lord following Percy's death reinforces the allusion (106-107). The reference is not surprising, in light of King's comment to Michael J. Bandler of the <u>Chicago Tribune Book World</u> that Golding's novel provided one of the most frightening experiences King ever had in reading a book ("Stephen King," <u>Contemporary Authors</u> 34), or his use of Golding's name "Castle Rock" in stories and novels (<u>Castle Rock</u> #4).

The coldness of fate is suggested by a deft reference to Thornton Wilder. A sudden storm washes out a bridge; the Walkers look forward to a forced halt, only to discover that the military Squads have thrown up a hasty replacement. As the Walkers cross it, one calls it "The Bridge of San Loois Ray" (68), adding his forlorn hope that it may yet fall. It does not; and by standing, it leads as irrevocably to death as had Wilder's collapsing bridge.

In the final pages of the novel, King conjures up the shade of Conrad to lend the novel even greater evocative power. After the hideous suffering the Walkers endure, after the agonies of four days of uninterrupted walking, with death the immediate result of stopping, only three remain: McVries, Stebbins, and Ray Garraty. As McVries suddenly collapses, the writing becomes frantic, moving rapidly in a series of short phrases, depending heavily upon images that assert horror as Garraty screams at McVries. Within half a page, McVries is gone, after providing one of the main images of stability throughout the preceding 240 pages. Less than a page later, Stebbins falters. At first, Stebbins does not recognize Garraty. Then he reaches out and grabs Garraty's shirt. The crowd is furious at the interference, but "only Garraty was close enough to see the horror in Stebbins's eyes, the horror, the darkness, and only Garraty knew that Stebbins's grip was a last despairing reach for rescue" (243).

As Conrad's Kurtz had realized, "The horror. The horror." After experiencing vicariously the suffering in The Long Walk and coming to understand precisely how meaningless it is, we can empathize with King's characters more fully . . . and with Conrad's.

The sense of horror is counterbalanced and intensified, if that were possible, by a touch of Tolkien and the epic quest. The Long Walk parodies the quest, using traditional motifs to emphasize the meaninglessness of this journey. On the first page of "Part III: The Rabbit," however, King notes that there are only "nine Walkers" left, reminding us of Tolkien's Nine Walkers sent out to combat the Ring Wraiths. The interminable march of Frodo and Sam across the wastes of Mordor bears a startling similarity to the Long Walk, but Tolkien's quest counts for something: Frodo and Sam destroy the Ring of Power and, for better or worse, bring an end to their age in Middle Earth. The last nine Walkers of The Long Walk have no such hope. They finish their parodic quest only when all are dead but one, and that one is helpless to change things.

The novel gains in interest and depth through King's allusions. But all of this is just dress rehearsal before the play . . . preparations for King's implicit homage to Shirley Jackson.

King establishes early in the novel that he has Jackson's stories in mind. Late the first night, as the Walkers pass through a small Maine town, King describes the buildings, the inhabitants, the atmosphere, then adds that Garraty "felt as if he had just walked through a Shirley Jackson short story" (77).

That King might structure a novel after one of Jackson's most famous short stories seems appropriate. His comments in Danse Macabre about her Haunting of Hill House imply that the Overlook Hotel might owe its genesis in part to her haunted house: The house may look normal enough, without any of the accouterments of horror, but it kills (256). Viewed in this light, <u>The Shining</u> on some levels reflects Jackson´s imagination. And less than three years after the publication of <u>The Long Walk</u>, King re-emphasized his debt to Jackson by dedicating <u>Firestarter</u> to her memory.

This interest in Jackson is central to <u>The Long Walk</u>. That isolated Maine town reminded Garraty of a Jackson short story because he has become involved in such a story--King´s own extension of "The Lottery."

In <u>Danse Macabre</u>, King discusses "The Lottery." Horror tales, he says, are essentially and often unconsciously symbolic. One of the symbolic values implicit in horror is its assurance that it is "okay to destroy the outsider," to become one with the unthinking mob. The prime example, he continues, is "The Lottery," where the outsider is identified by the purely arbitrary device of a black spot on a white paper (43). Someone gives little Davie Hutchinson a few small stones; Tess Hutchinson stands at the center of the mob. "It isn´t fair," she cries. Old Man Warner, Steve Adams (almost A-Z), and the grotesquely named Mrs. Graves stand at the front of the crowd. "It isn´t fair, it isn´t right," Mrs. Hutchinson screamed, and then they were upon her" (Jackson 302).

The final phrase accurately describes the students´ responses to Ted Jones in <u>Rage</u>. King evokes Jackson even more directly, however, in repeating the phrase "It´s not fair" throughout <u>The Long Walk</u>. Mrs. Hutchinson says it twice within half-a-dozen lines; Walkers repeat it also, invariably at points parallelling Jackson´s uses in "The Lottery."

Midway through Chapter 2, one of the Walkers, Curley, is struck with a leg cramp. In a sentence as breathless as the event it describes, King writes: "The crowd gasped, as if they hadn´t known this was the way it was, and the Walkers gasped, as if they hadn´t known, and Garraty gasped with them, but of course he had known, of course they had all known, it was very simple, Curley was going to get his ticket." Like Mrs. Hutchinson, Curley is suddenly alone in the middle of a cleared space, suddenly aware of what is to happen, and screams, "It isn't fair!" The motif repeats in Chapter 10 when Olson is gut-shot as punishment for turning on the soldiers guarding the Walkers. Garraty cradles the body, then is pulled away by McVries. Again, "It isn't fair!" Scramm, the odds-on favorite, catches a cold that rapidly develops into pneumonia, virtually insuring his death. "It isn't fair," Garraty repeats, shocked; Scramm has become a person to him, rather than just a number.

Connections between The Long Walk and "The Lottery" extend much deeper than one repeated phrase, however. The lottery begins at 10:00 AM on June 27, although preparations had begun earlier. In The Long Walk, preparations culminate in a lottery on national television to select the one hundred Walkers and one hundred alternates. Jackson's lottery is connected with fertility rites, reflected in Old Man Warner's doggerel, "Lottery in June, corn be heavy soon" (297). King does not make quite such an explicit connection between lottery and fertility rite, although the Long Walk does begin at 9:00 AM on May 1, a date King associates in The Eyes of the Dragon with a celebration of the spring planting.

Jackson's village represents a microcosm of society as a whole. Steve Adams draws first for himself and his family; Zanini draws last, symbolically completing the range of humanity. In The Long Walk, Aaronson receives Number 1 from the Major; Number 100 is a boy named Zuck. As with Jackson's lottery, King's is irrevocable. Past a specified date, no one may withdraw or change his mind. In a previous Walk, one boy froze at the starting line; he was given his three warnings, then shot down at 9:02 without his having taken a step. Jackson's lottery has become a ritual, its original meanings lost in time. There was at one time, we are told, a ritual chant by a minor functionary standing in a certain pose, and a ritual salute, also lost over the years. The box itself is almost talismanic, a dull black, worn by time; it had replaced the original box long before the memory of Old Man Warner, the oldest participant.

King's lottery is equally freighted with ritual. It has become surrounded by legend--this Long Walk made it into Massachusetts, that was won by a local boy. The boys become cult objects almost worshiped by the crowd, their cast-off shoes, their used food concentrates, even their excrement collected and treasured. In both lotteries, the participants cease to be human beings and become instead lambs for the slaughter.

There are, of course, differences. Jackson's lottery is far more restricted in scope, encompassing a few hours in a single village of three hundred people. King's is televised nationwide, with billions in wagers riding on the outcome. Although there are only one hundred Walkers, the entire society is involved as spectators, directly or indirectly. Jackson's lottery suggests momentarily that the children are in as much danger as the adults; little Dave Hutchinson must take his turn drawing from the box. Finally, however, Jackson allows the mother to suffer for her family. In spite of Tessie Hutchinson's attempts to include her married daughter in the drawing, she chooses the fatal lot and is killed. Someone, Jackson notes, gives Davy a few pebbles.

In <u>The Long Walk</u>, King's vision is more threatening. Adults do not run any risk at all. Walkers must be under nineteen; adults not only fail to protect children but actively urge the boys to their deaths. As close as the similarities between "The Lottery" and <u>The Long Walk</u> may be, this single difference is sufficient to suggest that King is moving well beyond Jackson's world.

In addition, Jackson's lottery in some sense completes a purpose. It stimulates the crops, Old Man Warner asserts. The north village may disband the lottery, he continues, but if so, the villagers will find themselves living in caves and eating chickweed stew. The Long Walk, on the other hand, serves no apparent purpose.

This is not entirely true, of course. The repressive, militaristic government King alludes to thrives on the Walk, a futuristic version of the Roman "bread and circuses" and an opportunity for the Major (who is rarely defined beyond that title) to be seen and applauded. It is a crime to speak out against the Walk, as Garraty knows from experience; his father was "squaded" for not holding his tongue. Business must defer to the Walkers. Dogs who interfere with the Walkers are shot down. Even bystanders interfering with them are liable to arrest and possible death. On the surface, the Walk appears to play some vital role in King's future society.

Beneath that appearance lies the reality, but only Walkers understand that reality. One by one they are shot; even if they are already dead, they are ritualistically given their warnings, then shot through the head. As McVries notes throughout, only by dying can they understand the ultimate futility of the Walk . . . and then it is too late. Initially, each believes with Garraty that others might die, but he will not. As the walk continues, however, Garraty discovers that they are walking dead men waiting for the final bullet. They have, as McVries puts it, sold their souls for trivialities. The uselessness of their deaths and consequently of their truncated lives serves no function beyond providing momentary entertainment for Crowd, which packs the highway for the last miles, moaning in dissatisfaction when a Walker falters and recovers, cheating Crowd of a death.

This lack of purpose is perhaps the greatest disparity between Jackson's vision and King's. Hers terrifies in its quick brutality but at least hints of something resulting from the sacrifice. King's stultifies with page after page of suffering, unrelieved by the faintest suggestion of value. Although the novel contains no explicitly supernatural horror, it is horrific nonetheless, as it forces the reader to watch the physical, psychological, emotional, and finally spiritual disintegration of the Walkers.

Beyond that, the Long Walk becomes a symbolic analogue to life itself. It encompasses everyone from $\underline{A}$ to $\underline{Z}$. Once begun, it cannot be halted short of death. And in the end, everyone dies but one.

In Chapter 3, Garraty wonders about the old tale of a drowning man's life passing before him at the moment of death. He speculates on the possibility that the Walkers might similarly live the rest of their lives while on the Walk, including those parts they had not yet experienced. McVries distracts Garraty with an offer of a cigarette, but Garraty's unanswered question structures much of the novel. Given the range of emotions and experiences the Walkers endure, the answer seems to be "yes." Later, toward the end of the first day, Garraty notes how carefully the Walkers try to preserve the outward semblances of normal life. McVries brushes his teeth after eating his concentrates; others wave to the crowds because that is the polite thing to do. After all, one of the functions of civilization is to ensure polite interaction between individuals.

As the hours and days wear on, Garraty begins to feel that they have been on the road forever, that there is nothing else besides the Walk. Even the crowds fade into the background, only intermittently disturbing the Walkers' progress toward death. By the fourth day, Baker talks about how difficult it is to keep his mind under control. He continually thinks about the past: favorite books, favorite summer pastimes, his first girlfriend. He thinks about such things more and more, he complains, as if he were "old and gettin' senile" (211).

By the last day, however, all that remains is the image of death itself. Garraty visualizes death as a state. He sees himself lying silently in a dusty room, with no worries, no pain, no relationships at all. Just nothing. "An end to the agony of movement," he thinks, "to the long nightmare of going down the road" (226).

As King details the Walkers' deaths, he creates horror within reality and defines the Long Walk as allegory, beginning arbitrarily, continuing through pain and discomfort, and ending in dissolution. The novel explores a range of possibilities. Death comes quietly for some; several of the Walkers simply faint, and while they lay unconcious the soldiers give them their warnings and shoot them. There is no pain, no fear, only cessation of pain. Others try to escape death. Under the apparent cover of darkness, Percy edges toward the surrounding forest, forfeiting his life the instant he leaves the pavement. For a moment, it looks as if he might escape. He is within a step or two of concealing shrubbery, the focus of surreptitious attention from all of the Walkers. At the last second, the rifles open fire. It had all been an illusion. The guards, with their sophisticated tracking equipment, had known where he was and what he was attempting. They had merely played with him.

For others, death is more violent. Olson dies of a symbolic cancer, devoured from within by his own fear. He sinks deeper and deeper into himself, until he becomes an ambulant corpse, responding to nothing. He eats at himself, at his body's reserves, functioning just below consciousness. Finally, there is nothing left. When he rouses at last, he is scarcely capable of speech; he can barely move. But he finds the energy to attack the soldiers. Gut-shot, he struggles to continue the Walk, his life pouring out between his fingers. His is a painful, messy death.

Barkowitz goes one step further. Throughout, he has played the cynic, the irritant, goading at least one Walker to his death. For that, he is ostracized, even within the frighteningly small community of the Walk. He walks on hatred, feeding his strength with each insult and each pain. For several chapters, the other Walkers expect him to fall, but he does not. Then, suddenly, with one clawing gesture, he rips his throat out. Even in a context McVries describes as ritual suicide, Barkovitch's is a true self-murder.

Scramm and Mike (one of two Hopi brothers on the Walk) face death more philosophically. Scramm develops pneumonia; Mike gets stomach cramps. Both know that they must die. They say farewell to their friends, then together walk to the side of the road. After a single rude salute to the guards, they sit and begin talking to one another.

The crowds pull away, knowing what must come. The remaining Walkers pass and do not look back.

Baker, already mentioned as feeling senile, dies of what can only be defined as old age. Others go insane and are shot down without ever feeling the bullets passing through their bodies. And it goes on. One hundred boys. Ninety-nine variants on death.

In the end, they all die. Death is the final destination on the life-journey.

Of course, the Long Walk is largely symbolic or allegorical. After all, it is only a game in the context of the novel, a competition in which the winner receives The Prize: anything and everything he wants, for life. And there is always a winner.

Or is there? The boys discuss The Prize frequently, joking first about what they will choose, then more realistically about what they would have chosen. Gradually, however, they realize how small a chance each has of winning. Then the discussion shifts. Has there ever really been a winner? McVries says no, that the surviving Walker is taken quietly behind a barn and shot. After all, the Walk itself is ritualized death, and no one can escape death.

What little background we receive about the Walk does nothing to change this impression. Garraty recalls the one Maine boy ever to win the Walk. Nearly blind and crippled by the end of the Walk, he died within the week. Even the conclusion of the novel is ambiguous. Within three pages of the end, there are still three Walkers. Two die quickly. Even before the soldiers can fire the ritual shots through the already dead Stebbins´ head, a jeep pulls onto the road. The Major stands up, saluting, ready to grant The Prize.

But Garraty walks past him, unseeing almost, uncaring. A hand rests on his shoulder. He walks on: "The dark figure beckoned, beckoned in the rain, beckoned for him to come and walk, to come and play the game . . . . There was still so far to walk" (244).

In the end, death awaits even the victor.

Allegory in horror, King says, is "built-in, a given, impossible to escape" (<u>Danse Macabre</u> 43). Through it we speak symbolically about things we fear to approach directly. The Long Walk as life-journey allows King an image by which to examine and criticize society. The novel is violent, graphic and explicit. King will spend several paragraphs on a Walker's death agony, or several pages in Olson's case, as the boy struggles to Walk, clutching at his own intestines through an open wound in his belly. The violence creates its own horror, critical to King's purposes.

In "Horror and the Limits of Violence," King defines excessive violence as action dissociated from morality. A nail driven gratuitously through a thumbnail could constitute unnecessary violence, because the pain inflicted is gratuitous. "As far as violence goes," he continues, "I will write what I see, and trust that the context of the story is strong enough so that the violence is part of it, and therefore moral" (<u>Shadowings</u> 129).

That presupposition is important in <u>The Long Walk</u>. Although the novel highlights violence of many sorts, all leading to death, it is an intensely moral book. As did <u>Rage</u>, <u>The Long Walk</u> concentrates on the adolescent in society, anatomizing the failure of structures theoretically designed to support and protect the child.

In the context of the novel, only the Walkers fully understand what the Walk entails. Garraty himself had seen a portion of the Walk; intellectually he had registered the pain and isolation of the boys, but emotionally, he could not. Like the others, and most specifically like the adults surrounding him, he saw the Walk as a species of competition, a game.

King virtually forces the readers to note the implicit disparity between the two views of the Walk, the participants' and the spectators'. For the spectators, it is largely a game like the television game shows central to <u>The Running Man</u>. It is a spectacle for national consumption, something on which one might bet, something for which one might stay awake until midnight just to see the Walkers pass through town. King makes explicit the correlation between Walk and Game through the headnotes to his chapters. Chapter 1 begins with a quotation from Groucho Marx's <u>You Bet Your Life</u>. The irony, of course, is that this is precisely what the Walkers have done, although none of them quite realize it yet. Chapter 2, which details the opening miles of the Walk and the coalescing relationships among the Walkers, has a similarly ironic headnote, a quotation from Monty Hall's <u>Let's Make a Deal</u>. For Chapter 3, it is Art Fleming and <u>Jeopardy</u>; for Chapter 4, Chuck Barris and <u>The Gong Show</u>. This headnote deserves quotation in full, since it defines the connections between <u>The Long Walk</u> and <u>The Running Man</u>: "The ultimate game show would be one where the losing contestant was killed." The pattern continues until Chapter 8, which opens with a quotation from a child's rhyme. While not a reference to a game show, it emphasizes the surface triviality of the Walk.

Chapter 9 returns to television, juxtaposing Allen Ludden and <u>College Bowl</u> with <u>Sesame Street</u>'s Count Count in Chapter 10. The remaining chapter headnotes create a continuous ironic counterpoint to the episodes, becoming more impelling as the nature of the games involved becomes more serious. One headnote refers to the Liston-Ali title fight, another to Vince Lombardi and football, a third to World War I.

"Part III: The Rabbit" balances "Part I: Starting Out." Both contain two chapters; both establish critical tones. Part I opened the novel with references to Groucho Marx and Monty Hall. Part III concludes it with references to ultimate games in which contestants do die. Chapter 17 quotes Jim Jones, recalling the incredible events in Guyana. Chapter 18 quotes the Major, linking the real world of children's rhymes, television game shows, football games, world wars, and mass murder/suicides with the fictitious world of the Long Walk. The Major becomes "real" by association, and the Walk culminates our obsession with vicarious danger.

This game, however, is for real, just as the game Charlie Decker and the other students played in _Rage_ was for real. The prize is adulthood, maturity, a place within society. The only problem is that the contestants do not understand the rules until too late. They believe with Garraty that when the first Walker falters, the guards will point their rifles and pull the triggers. The rifles will spurt little flags reading "Bang," then everyone will have a good laugh and go home. By the time they know differently, they cannot turn back.

Again as in _Rage_, _The Long Walk_ examines several levels of support, concluding that all ultimately fail. If the Long Walk is a game, it is one devised by society. Yet society itself proves unappealing as it is revealed to the Walkers. Initially, Garraty and the others respond to onlookers as one might expect. The Walkers are shy, waving occasionally, flushing when someone pays them specific attention--a constant problem for Garraty, since he is from Maine and therefore the local favorite. Gradually, though, the Walkers´ attitudes alter. The crowd becomes the Crowd, a faceless, amorphous entity surrounding them, urging them to their deaths. Stebbins recalls the final miles of a previous Walk; people were packed sixty deep for fifty miles. Twenty people were crushed to death. McVries reminds Garraty at one point that two billion dollars in bets ride on which Walker dies when. Later, Garraty and McVries discuss the spectators as animals enjoying the spectacle of death. As Walkers falter and receive their tickets, the crowd´s responses become more overtly sexual, linking generation of life with destruction of life. To further emphasize the Walkers´ isolation, no one is allowed to give the Walkers any food or water; physical contact is possible only as long as the Walker remains on the road and is willing to collect Warnings for every moment´s delay.

King´s indictment of society is not limited to the spectators, however. As the Walk progresses, the boys form loosely knit groups, small communities that provide companionship and comfort. They talk, sing, keep each other´s spirits up. Occasionally they act against their own best interests to keep others alive. After all, the sooner everyone else is dead, the sooner the winner achieves his Prize. McVries twice rescues Garraty within seconds of death; Garraty repays McVries, risking his own life each time. When it becomes evident that Scramm will not complete the Walk, the boys pledge that the winner will support Scramm's wife and unborn child. The sense of internal community is important to the Walkers. Everything else has failed, and the alternative is total isolation from everyone. As Stebbins says, probably every Long Walk finds its cause to support, and probably just at this point, "when the old realities and mortalities begin to sink in" (Ch. 12).

Even this rudimentary community breaks down, however. When Garraty sees his mother and his girlfriend, he loses control; only McVries' interference saves his life. Shortly thereafter, Abraham approaches Garraty with a proposition. From now on, they agree, there can be no more interference. Walkers must live or die by their own actions and choices. As their number dwindles, it becomes harder to help others, when doing so only increases the suffering of all. To that extent, their isolation becomes complete. Garraty breaks through the isolation in the end, but it is too late. Everyone he feels any remaining attachment for is dead.

Society and community are not King's only targets in the novel. As he does elsewhere, he also investigates the family. Because of the nature of the novel, he focuses less intently on family here than he did in <u>Rage</u> or would do in <u>Christine</u> when Arnie Cunningham bluntly asserts that "part of being a parent is trying to kill your kids" (26). Parents serve virtually no function in the novel. Garraty's mother drives him to the starting point, then effectively disappears until a brief episode toward the end, when Garraty sees her and his girlfriend Jan in the crowd. Garraty virtually ignores his mother, both in this episode and in his reminiscences. She is a cipher, too weak to support him, too apathetic to talk him out of the Walk. The only other mother visible in the novel is a variant on the monster-mother of Rage. Percy's mother shows up several times, trying to break through police cordons to help her boy. She is overprotective in all but what counts--he is a Walker and doomed to die.

Fathers are equally weak. Unlike Carl Decker, Garraty's father does not hate his son. He merely proves incapable of supporting him. Garraty's father is weak, afraid to take a stand against the government, yet unable to hold his tongue when he is drunk. He speaks against the Walk and disappears.

One father, however, recurs throughout the novel: the Major. He is a consistent father-image, representing a paternalistic regime that finds the diversion of the Long Walk necessary to retain its power. At the beginning, the Major inspires the boys, demanding their awe and respect. Yet in the first chapter, before Garraty defines and accepts his own father's limitations, he remembers his father's comment that the Major was "the rarest and most dangerous monster any nation [could] produce, a society-supported sociopath." As the Walk continues, the Walkers turn against the Major, speaking of him with contempt, using him as the butt of obscene jokes. But when he drives by, they find themselves cheering him, saluting him in spite of their new awareness.

In the end, King suggests that the Major is even more of a monster than Garraty or his father suspected. Stebbins reveals that he is one of the Major's many bastard sons. He gives no proof for his statement, and by that time, he is well on the way toward insanity; but his contempt for the Major shows through clearly. He entered the Walk, he says, to prove himself to his father: his Prize will be a place in his father's home. But he finally realizes that he has been used. He is the rabbit after which Part III is named, the mechanical device that runs ahead of the dogs to spur them on. Only in this case, the rabbit has discovered that it too is flesh and blood . . . and can die. The paternalistic Major in effect

collaborates in the death of his own son.
   If neither society nor parents can provide support for the Walkers, they must rely on themselves. Unfortunately, few of them are well enough adjusted, or fully enough matured emotionally and psychologically to stand on their own. Walker after Walker falls prey to an inner monster, to a fear or need that undermines him and finally kills him. Many of the Walkers are identified only by brief external clues: one whimpers that he wants to go home, another cries incessantly until he falls and is shot, still another collapses under the pressure of religious mania.
   Several Walkers display greater strength, however. Since the novel depends more upon character and interaction than upon traditional plot, the individuals become critical. McVries grows stronger through much of the novel, as his cynicism wears away and he can speak about his own past. Stebbins' silence endures for much of the novel; eventually, however, he too admits his own weaknesses, masters them, and moves beyond them. Barkovitch exists on hatred, Olson on self-delusion.
   Garraty is the most important of the characters, of course, and the most difficult. He stands at the center of the novel. Although <u>The Long Walk</u> avoids the dangers of a first-person narrator, it does focus on Garraty. We see him arriving at the starting point. We meet other Walkers as Garraty meets them. It is, therefore, no surprise that Garraty survives; the point of the novel is less who wins The Prize than what happens to all of them in the process of trying.
   Garraty is a more complex character than the others. He is less confident than Stebbins or McVries or Scramm, less aware of his own motivation than Barkovitch, less capable of folding in on himself than Olson. And perhaps that is his greatest strength. Unlike the others, he does not depend upon a single attribute to carry him through. Scramm, for instance, is physically more capable than anyone else in the race, but when he catches a cold he is doomed. Each of the other

Walkers has a secret strength, a source of ultimate identity, and when it is depleted, he dies.

Garraty lives with more dimensions of self. He lacks the confidence the others have. True, he cannot visualize himself dying, being shot in the head, but neither can he see himself winning. Even more, he accepts changes and adapts to them. When the weather shifts or the sun sets or a friend gets his ticket, Garraty rebounds. His reactions may hurt him and occasionally bring him close to death, but he can pull away. His closest approach to death occurs when he sees his mother and Jan. Even there, however, when everything in him tells him to stay with them, to touch them, even though the guards have called out his third warning and he has only seconds before the rifles fire, he finds the strength to survive. McVries pulls at him; Jan pleads with him to leave. But when he acts, it is through his own choice. Garraty walks away alone, telling McVries to let go of him.

Garraty's strength lies in his ambiguous relationships with others and within himself. King suggests Garraty's fundamental insecurity by using the same motif of sexuality he had used so effectively in <u>Rage</u>. Unlike Charlie Decker, Ted Jones, and others in <u>Rage</u>, Garraty is a virgin. He wants to experience sex. He embraces a girl, willingly taking his warnings in exchange for a few seconds of intimacy. Later, he daydreams about Jan, vowing to stay faithful to her and not to wave at any more girls. Gribble's frustrating and disastrous sexual encounter leads to Garraty's own orgasm within seconds of Gribble's death. And, along with the other Walkers, much of what he says and thinks is sexual in nature.

But his sexuality, like everything else in his personality, has not yet been fully defined. Because he is a virgin, he fears that he may be homosexual, in spite of his clear attachment to Jan. Again and again, he refers to homosexuality, at first as a stereotypic jibe directed at other Walkers, then more seriously as he recalls and tries to submerge memories of playing "doctor" with another boy, Jim, and his mother's threat that she would make him run naked through the street. In effect, the threat has come true in the Walk. He is not naked, but he must perform his bodily functions in full sight of Crowd.

The image of Jim and their play recurs most critically when Garraty is sexually aroused by memories of Jan or by events surrounding him. As the Walk progresses, he becomes more and more unsure of himself, largely because of McVries. In the beginning, McVries seems the stronger, the more self-assured, yet he speaks to Garraty in an oddly effeminate tone: "You're a dear boy," he says, leaving Garraty "to walk alone, feeling more confused than ever" (27). McVries continues to tease Garraty, blowing him a kiss, telling Garraty he could "get horny" for him, calling Garraty "sweet," yet without coming across as overtly homosexual. The innuendoes are just sufficient to make Garraty worry about his own sexuality. By the end of Chapter 8, Garraty notes that both Jimmy and McVries have scars, then remembers himself and Jimmy playing doctor. Then comes the rumor that the two Hopis, Mike and Jim, are "queer for each other," a rumor Garraty dismisses. They do not seem effeminate at all, he decides, not that it is any of his business.

The motif of homosexuality culminates in Chapter 14. McVries tells Garraty that Parker, one of the remaining Walkers, thinks they are "queer for each other." Garraty responds with outrage, but McVries is thoughtful. "Maybe he's even half right. Maybe that's why I saved your ass. Maybe I'm queer for you." Garraty tries to laugh the comment off as a joke, but McVries shocks him further: "Would you let me jerk you off?"

Garraty's response provides the rationale for the sequence of references. McVries may be joking; he is not even going to tell Garraty whether he is or is not. But more critically, Garraty <u>wants</u> to be touched, not sexually, but physically. The isolation of the Walk is so intense that even sexuality becomes irrelevant. All that matters is human contact.

McVries shocks Garraty into examining his own motives. Later, when Stebbins uses a homosexual jibe to disconcert Garraty, Garraty can ignore it. His memories of Jimmy, coupled with his experiences with McVries, provide him with enough self-awareness that Stebbins´ efforts at psychological warfare fail. Through the Long Walk, Garraty matures beyond an adolescent obsession with sexuality to accept the Walkers, even himself, for what they are. The touches of homosexuality in the novel never fully develop; it is possible that McVries was in fact joking all along. But they do allow Garraty to confront and overcome his own confusions, and by doing so develop the strength to endure.

In several ways, <u>The Long Walk</u> is atypical of King´s fictions. Like <u>Rage</u>, it is almost without plot: ninety-nine boys walk until they cannot walk any longer, then they are shot. And like <u>Rage</u>, it depends heavily upon characterization through dialogue and reminiscence. Stylistically, it is unusually restrained. The novel is shorter than his usual, verbally more precise, less dependent on "brand-names" and parenthetical or italicized interruptives. It creates the illusion of horror, but without recourse to supernatural horror itself. True horror, as King would illustrate so ably in "The Last Rung on the Ladder" or "The Body" can be implicit in this world.

At the same time, it does connect with works published under King´s name. The setting is typically King. He re-creates the route of the Long Walk as precisely as if he were working with a map of Maine, New Hampshire, and Massachusetts. As in so many of his short stories and novels, the landscape becomes almost a character, at times deceptively calm, at times openly destructive. There are touches of autobiography in Garraty´s father´s disappearance and in what seems a reference to King´s responses to the paperback sale of <u>Carrie</u>. Garraty tries to explain the evanescence of life by asking Baker "what if you spent the next six weeks planning what you were going to do with the cash--never mind the Prize, just the cash--and what if the first time you went out to buy something, you got flattened by a taxicab" (41). King's response to his $400,000 advance for <u>Carrie</u> was almost identical. He decided to buy his wife a present, but feared that as he crossed a street,

> a drunk would come along in a car and things would be put back in perspective . . . . I scuttled across those streets, looking both ways. Because I was really convinced that that was going to be the payback, like in those E. C. Comics. (Winter, "Stephen King's Art of Darkness" 15)

<u>The Long Walk</u> also contains several images King would later incorporate into short stories published under his own name. A reference to Wednesday night Bingo, with a coverall prize of a twenty-pound turkey, suggests "The Word Processor." The guards sitting under an umbrella on the half-track, while the Walkers struggle through the mid-day heat, suggests "Dolan's Cadillac," a 1985 short story published serially in <u>Castle Rock</u>.

The second of the Bachman novels, then, continues the movement of the first. While still identifiably a product of King's imagination, it works in new territory, connecting with King's other works through shared settings, themes, characters, and consistent criticism of society and social relationships. It is a strong novel, intriguing in character and episode. Like <u>Rage</u>, it repays a second and third reading, increasing in depth and complexity as the reader becomes involved in it.

NOTES

[1] Leonard Heldreth organized the session. The

other papers included Anthony S. Magistrale's "Stephen King's Vietnam Allegory: An Interpretation of 'Children of the Corn,'" later published in The Cuyahoga Review, 2 (Spring/Summer 1984) 61-66; Michael Collings' "Stephen King's The Stand: Science Fiction into Fantasy"; Mary Ferguson's "Strawberry Spring: Stephen King's Gothic Universe"; and Dennis O'Donovan's "Monster Love: or Why Is Stephen King." Douglas Winter served as respondent. (The articles by Hatlen, Magistrale, and Ferguson, were reprinted in Footsteps V [April 1985].)

Hatlen's other articles include "Alumnus Publishes Symbolic Novel, Shows Promise," in The Maine Campus, 12 April 1974; "'Salem's Lot Critiques American Civilization," in The Maine Campus, 12 December 1975; "Steve King's The Stand," in Kennebec, April 1979; and "Steve King's Third Novel Shines On," in The Maine Campus, 1 April 1977.

Chapter V

ROADWORK

With <u>Roadwork</u>, the Bachman novels shift content and approach. <u>Rage</u> and <u>The Long Walk</u> were adolescent novels in several senses: they were written in part while King was a student; they center on adolescents caught in an uncaring or antithetical society; they share a directness and simplicity of structure and narrative movement that suggest apprenticeship pieces rather than mature novels.

These characteristics correlate with what King was publishing under his own name. <u>Carrie</u> provides a nearly perfect analogue to <u>Rage</u>, the primary difference being the infusion of horror elements into the former. <u>'Salem's Lot</u> places children in the middle of the action, while simultaneously dissolving most family ties. <u>The Shining</u> carries this approach to its extreme, isolating the basic family unit of father, mother, and child. The father becomes the primary threat, with the child surviving only by the death of the parent.

In <u>The Stand</u>, King shifts his attention to adults. Although their world remains inimical to children (adults developed the superflu virus, after all), the novel concentrates on adult interactions. It also concludes more optimistically than the earlier novels, with the birth of a child and the restructuring of the family around Stu Redman and Fanny Goldsmith. <u>The Dead Zone</u> further restricts its actions to Johnny Smith's experiences. At the conclusion, he literally sacrifices himself to save a child, reversing the movement of most of the earlier novels.

This emphasis on the adult first appears in the Bachman novels with <u>Roadwork</u>, in Barton George Dawes' attempts to save his marriage, his home, his business, his pride, and his identity from destruction by a bureaucratic, profit-oriented society--a theme continued in both The Running Man and Thinner. They are adult novels as well in their increasingly complex plotting and characterization. Backgrounds expand to include more than a single classroom in Placerville High School or the highway of the Long Walk; characters interact more completely with the others in more demanding situations.

The last three Bachman novels also seem more mature in style and treatment. One of the difficulties in working with the Bachman novels is identifying which might have been the unpublished novels King has referred to as his earliest attempts. Winter mentions a "first novel-length manuscript"; a first "true novel"; a second novel, Sword in the Darkness; a third novel, Getting It On; and a fourth, unnamed novel as preceeding Carrie (The Art of Darkness xvi-xvii).

In a 1981 interview, however, King gave a slightly different list. Before Carrie, he wrote Getting It On, presumably his earliest novel, since he refers to it first; Babylon Here; and a race riot novel, Sword of the Darkness that was "just terrible. After that, I started to get it together; I did Carrie and ´Salem´s Lot, and the other stuff came right along." Two of the novels, he continues, were rejected by publishers; the third "just seemed Dead On Arrival" (Stewart 45-46).

From King´s descriptions, it seems likely that Getting It On was an early title for Rage, given the frequency of the phrase "getting it on" in the novel; King´s secretary, Stephanie Leonard, recently confirmed that supposition (Letter). The Long Walk, which King referred to in the Bangor Daily News interview as having been completed during his first year in college, does not fit any of the descriptions provided here, however.

There is thus some confusion as to when and in what order King wrote the Bachman novels. A recent article in Publishers Weekly, written after King´s interview in the Bangor Daily News and presumably incorporating the most authoritative information available, states that the first four were "written while King was in high school and college, but only made available for publication much later" ("Bachman Revealed" 43). The article also describes the four as more science fiction than horror.

Those conclusions certainly fit The Long Walk. Castle Rock says that King wrote it while still in college; and its setting in a paternalistic, near-future United States could qualify it as science fiction, although there are few of the technological innovations readers of SF might expect. Rage fits less securely. According to Castle Rock, the first forty pages were written while King was in high school; presumably it could have been completed while King was in college, but the novel had to have been revised before publication, since it refers to films produced in 1974 and 1975.

Roadwork, however, does not fit at all. Given its subtitle, "A Novel of the First Energy Crisis," and its narration of events between November 20, 1973 and January 20, 1974, it is difficult to see how it could have been written while King was in college. Nor is it in any meaningful sense science fiction. It is almost entirely mainstream, outlining Dawes´ responses to rapidly altering, if not disintegrating social conditions in the America of 1974; with its publication date of 1981 and King´s accurate re-creation of then-current conditions, the novel cannot be classified as science fiction. Its emphasis on a single adult, a husband and father incapable of protecting his family from the world we know, suggests more The Stand, Firestarter, or Cujo than Carrie. While it might have been completed earlier than 1981, it seems unlikely that it was written more than a decade before.

In addition, one other piece of internal evidence argues for a completion date later than 1972. As he had done in Rage and The Long Walk, King includes several literary references in Roadwork, unusual in this novel since, unlike the first two, it does not deal directly with American educational systems. Even a cursory look at the allusions suggests that Roadwork relates to mainstream American literature. King mentions fantasy or horror writers: Poe and Lovecraft (although not until later chapters, when Barton Dawes´ life has become a living horror), Kurt Vonnegut, Lewis Carroll, Franz Kafka, and H. Rider Haggard. The name "Ridpath" (44) and a pin in the shape of an owl suggest Peter Straub´s Shadowland, published a year before Roadwork, while King and Straub were working on The Talisman; the nature of the reference makes it likely that King borrowed them from Straub, not the reverse.

King also cites mainstream literary figures, however, enhancing the sense of Roadwork as social criticism rather than as horror or as fantasy. Shakespeare, Thomas Carlyle, O. Henry, John Dos Passos, Victoria Holt (in a context defining her negative literary worth), T.S. Eliot, and George Orwell all appear, giving the novel a texture unusual in Stephen King; it is as if the one-time English teacher has temporarily overshadowed the horror fantasist.

While most of these references are admittedly slight, they do prepare for more fully integrated allusions to Ernest Hemingway´s Nick Adams. These references are critical to the tone of Roadwork, literally framing King´s story. The name "Nick Adams" appears in the opening chapter and on the final page of the narrative, just before the "Epilogue." In between, King continually suggests themes and techniques Hemingway developed through Nick Adams.

The Nick Adams stories first appeared out of chronological sequence, two or three at a time in collections of short fiction. Not until 1972 were the stories published in the order of Nick Adams´ life, that is, just before King probably wrote Roadwork. That collection, The Nick Adams Stories (Scribner´s 1972), seems particularly relevant to the Bachman novels. The first tale, "Three Shots," one of eight previously unpublished pieces, tells an early episode in Nick Adam´s life. Its opening paragraph is startling when compared with a passage in Rage:

      Nick was undressing in the tent.

> He saw the shadows of his father and
> Uncle George cast by the fire on the
> canvas wall. He felt very uncomfortable
> and ashamed and undressed as fast as he
> could, piling his clothes neatly. (13)

Nick stays still, afraid to move, afraid of . . . something that suddenly transforms into fear of death. A few paragraphs later, he overhears his father and Uncle George discussing him, accusing him of being a coward and a liar. That experience echoes thematically and imagistically in the Nick Adams stories, just as Charlie's hunting trip with his father and his father's friends echoes throughout <u>Rage</u>. (Later, in <u>Cujo</u>, Charity Camber uses the promise of just such a hunting trip to persuade Joe Camber to let her take Brett to Connecticut). Even the specific images of shadows against a canvas wall and a boy lying immobilized by fear inside his tent repeat between "Three Shots" and <u>Rage</u>. Given that King had graduated from the University of Maine in 1970 with a degree in English and had taught English at Hampden Academy between 1971 and 1973, when <u>The Nick Adams Stories</u> was published, it seems probable that his fictional hunting trips reflect Hemingway's.

Although it might seem quibbling to insist upon this close a relationship between King and Hemingway, the fact remains that <u>Roadwork</u> parallels the Nick Adams stories. King himself has acknowledged a debt to Hemingway; the narrator of "The Body" refers to his story, "Stud City," as derivative and sophomoric, theme by Faulkner, style by Hemingway (<u>Different Seasons</u> 335). That King should acknowledge Hemingway's influence is not surprising, given Hemingway's impact American letters. According to Philip Young, Hemingway's influence was almost immeasurable for "well over a quarter of a century," particularly in those genres conventionally considered "subliterary." Young discusses detective fiction specifically, with its concentration on "pain, gore, brutality, evil and all-around toughness," a "travesty of Hemingway" incorporating surface characteristics while ignoring underlying purpose (200-201).

The Nick Adams stories, in turn, epitomize Hemingway's influence, especially "Big Two-Hearted River," a two-part story that concludes In Our Times. Its first critics called it a story in which nothing happens, a comment equally applicable (on the surface, at least) to either Rage or The Long Walk. Gradually, however, readers discovered beneath the static surface a dynamic narrative.

"Big Two-Hearted River" details Nick Adams' fishing trip shortly after the war. As a description of fishing, it is brilliant, but the story suggests even more. Everything Nick does is carefully detailed, as if the ritual of action is more important than the act itself. It seems that if the coffee is not prepared just so, or the grasshoppers threaded onto the hook just so, Nick will lose control. Young describes Nick's precise, mechanical actions as

> the mindless movements of, say, a woman who all alone busies herself with a thorough housecleaning on the morning after the sudden death of her husband, or the movements of the hands of a badly shell-shocked veteran who, while he can control himself, is performing simple jobs over and over in a factory: this, and then that. And then that and this. (46)

The irony is that Nick Adams is concerned with more than just the ritual of fishing. He has recently returned from war, where he had been seriously wounded. His nerves are as taut as the fishing line. Preserving his sanity is as dependent upon establishing and following rituals as is his success in catching fish. Hemingway imagistically equates Nick with a fish swimming against the current. It makes no headway; the best it can do is hold steady. Matthew Cowley, an early critic, described these rituals as providing an "escape from a nightmare or from realities that have become a nightmare" (Young 45).

In Roadwork, Barton George Dawes, like Nick

Adams, has been through psychic warfare. He has been emotionally wounded and is barely holding onto his sanity. He retains what control he can over his life by preserving, for as long as possible, the house where he and his wife lived and loved and in which his son died of cancer.

Although his wound is not physical, it is as deep and as distressing as was Nick Adams´. In Roadwork, King depends on the same sense of nightmare in the daylight that Hemingway created in "Big Two-Hearted River." The opening line of the "Prologue" immediately communicates ambivalence, tension, and pressure: "But Viet Nam was over and the country was getting on." King never explicitly defines what the initial word but opposes; the novel counterpoints an idea never stated but implicit throughout.

The connections with Nick Adams structure the first section of Roadwork, "November 20, 1974." The first line summarizes Hemingway´s theme in "Big Two-Hearted River": "He kept doing things without letting himself think about them. Safer that way." Dawes resembles Nick Adams, who felt as if he had "left everything behind, the need for thinking, the need to write, other needs" (In Our Time 134). Everything must be done by ritual, without thought.

As Dawes stops by a gun shop, he notices a newspaper headline: "SHAKY CEASE-FIRE HOLDS." For Dawes and for King, this headline becomes a critical leitmotif. In varying forms, it appears three times in the first chapter; there is indeed an internal "shaky cease-fire" that is about to erupt into violence and death. Dawes knows that he is ruining himself and his wife, yet cannot act otherwise. He has split into two personalities: George, the rational Dawes, the one who wants to find a new home to replace the one about to be destroyed by the construction of a new freeway extension; and Freddy, an alter-ego for Dawes´ dead son Charlie. This second Dawes represents the self-destruction that parallels the Hemingway mystique: when one can no longer live as one must, one simply ends it.

Even King´s style emphasizes the need for

order and control, creating a mantra against disintegration. King relies on the specific, the concrete. On one level, this results in the "brand name" style so completely associated with him that other writers now imitate and parody it, as in Paul Proch and Charles Kaufman's "Eggboiler," a spoof of Firestarter published in National Lampoon (May 1984). Like The Long Walk, Roadwork begins with a variation on that emphasis on the concrete. Dawes sees a sign, just as Garraty sees a message on a computer terminal. In each case, King mentions the message, then reproduces it. In Roadwork, Dawes

>was walking to the bus stop when he saw the sign that said:

>AMMO HARVEY'S GUN SHOP AMMO
>Remington Winchester Colt Smith & Wesson
>HUNTERS WELCOME

By itself, this structure seems innocuous. It becomes an important clue to authorship, however, when the reader remembers how frequently King uses the same technique. In Roadwork, as in King's other fictions, the technique telegraphs characters' mental states. Two paragraphs later, King repeats "the headline said:" followed by an indented, bold-face message. The pattern repeats on the next page, the next, and the next. In fact, he uses this structure at least forty-three times in the text of Roadwork. Dawes is obsessed by precision, by external controls. If he can read a thing, it exists for him. Objective, external data support Dawes in precisely the same way objective, externalized perception had supported Nick Adams. For Adams, any deviation from the pattern threatened imbalance: for Dawes, failing to note those literal signposts of reality threatens to overload his circuiting device, allowing Freddy control.

Unfortunately, the objective shades into the irrational as Dawes begins to imagine signposts that take on increasingly threatening meanings. After a worker named Johnny Walker is killed in an accident, reality shifts to unreality. Dawes again sees a sign, this time an imaginary one hanging below Johnny Walker's stuffed head on Steve Ordner's den wall. The plaque says:

> HOMO LAUNDROMAT
> November 28, 1973
> Bagged on the corner of Deakman (86)

The split-second image is an early indication of encroaching insanity. Later, the signs become even more threatening. As Dawes prepares for the final confrontation over his home, he buys a car battery from Sears:

> Written on the side of the battery were these words, printed in raised plastic:
>
> DIE-HARD (242)

Given the context of the novel, the irony can hardly be unintentional.

As is frequently the case in King's fictions, however, the individual's problems merely reflect his society's. Dawes has become schizoid, driven to insanity by the death of his son, by sudden changes in his world. Society is equally altered. If Dawes' great trauma is his son's death from cancer, society's is the sudden shocking lack of cheap energy. Dawes must adjust to his loss. His wife, Mary, manages to adjust with only a few problems. She drinks a bit more than before, cries in front of him more than before (like Althea Breakstone in Cujo). But she is essentially healthy. Dawes, however, cannot let loose. He cannot separate past from present, memory from experience. For him, his son still lives in viciously graphic dreams culminating in Charlie's death, in the constant dialogue between Freddy and George. "Every night," King writes, "it seemed he and his son got together in one dream or another. Barton George Dawes and Charles Frederick Dawes, reunited by the wonders of the subconscious mind" (105).

American society is similarly caught between

two states. Dawes' personal breakdown parallels larger breakdowns in economics, politics, and social structures, a theme begun in Rage and The Long Walk and concluded in The Running Man. In an early chapter, Dawes tells another worker at the Blue Ribbon Laundry about the old days. Ray and Don Tarkington ran the laundry back then, as they had done since its beginnings in 1926. They were, Dawes concedes, "paternalistic exploiters of the uneducated working man and woman" (28), especially as viewed by contemporary labor leaders. But they cared. They were real. Under the old management, the laundry was a living thing; individuals counted for something. If an employee made a mistake, Ray Tarkington might throw him against a door; he would also loan that same man the money to return to college and earn a degree, on the condition that he bring his knowledge back and improve the laundry.

Against this, Dawes sets the current management, a conglomerate that sees the Blue Ribbon Laundry solely as an entry on a balance sheet. Profit or loss count for everything; traditions, integrity, individual loyalty are nothing. Dawes refuses to accept this mentality. He chooses instead to destroy the laundry . . . and himself.

The laundry becomes a microcosm for society. "The bottom's falling out" (36), Steve Ordner complains, blaming the status of the stock market on Nixon's domino theory. The theory hadn't worked against the communists in Southeast Asia, Ordner comments, so Nixon just took it and applied it to the American economy. America is obsessed with a "throw-away" economy, with corporation mentality, with what Dawes calls the "Trained Dog Ethic" (112). After being trained to love energy-consuming commodities for decades, the American people will now be trained to hate them. Dawes does not object to conservation: he objects to the training that makes conservation psychologically mandatory.

Dawes' attitudes suggest another connection with Nick Adams. Constance Montgomery notes in her study of biographical elements in Hemingway's fictions that Hemingway was seriously wounded in

World War I, just before he wrote "Big Two-Hearted River." She cites Hemingway's friend, Carl Edgar, as saying that Hemingway had been "figuratively and literally shot to pieces. He seemed to have a tremendous need to express the things that he had felt and seen" (119). Hemingway chose to express those things through Nick Adams, shell-shocked, struggling to re-create order in an increasingly disordered world. "Big Two-Hearted River," Philip Young argues, presents "a picture of a sick man, and of a man who is in escape from whatever it is that made him sick. And Nick obviously knows what is the matter and what he must do about it and must not do. He must keep physically occupied, keep his hands busy; he must not think or he will be unable to sleep" (47).

King had no physical wound, of course, but he has shown repeatedly his concern over social issues. In the fall of 1977, four years after publishing Roadwork, King began work with Peter Straub on The Talisman. Straub says that The Talisman described what King calls "Reagan's America"; more significantly, for both King and Straub the "healing of Jack's mother is not the sole purpose of the boy's quest: the implicit mother figure of The Talisman is Mother Earth, defiled by the cancerlike spread of modern civilization" (Winter, "Quest" 68).

In Roadwork, King confronts this cancer, using the context of a mainstream novel. Cancer symbolizes the problems of society, and of Barton George Dawes specifically. A lump of cells the size of a walnut epitomizes all that is frightening in Dawes' world. The wife of a friend dies of cancer within three weeks; its speed is as terrifying as anything else. Healthy tissues suddenly become the body's own enemy, destroying as it invades. Charlie, of course, had died of a brain cancer. When Dawes speaks with Olivia Brenner on Christmas Day, he tells her that he has a "soul-cancer," an accurate description of what is happening to him. Later, he imagines standing outside Wally Hanmer's house and taking a EEG of the "gigantic, tumored Party Brain" inside (194). Cancer is the great terror.

On another level, though, that is not quite true. Cancer invades the individual, destroys the individual. The survivors suffer for a while, but they can recover. On a larger scale, however, cancer becomes a metaphor for disorder and sudden, intrusive death. As metaphor, it is not confined to the Bachman novels. In one form or another, cancer appears in most of King's fiction. It is the great horror, the true horror beside which vampires and haunted houses and werewolves seem momentary and imaginary. In novel after novel, story after story, characters are struck by cancer, or see friends and relatives dying from it. The Talisman, after all, revolves around Jack Sawyer's attempts to rescue his mother from a cancer.

Cancer as symbol and as contemporary, elusive horror is eminently appropriate in King's novels. Horror in King is frequently something inexplicable. It happens. People suffer and die. That is how life is.

"The Raft" is one of King's most graphic examples of this sense. Four people take an October swim out to a raft. No one knows they are there. No one else will come along, since it is long past the season for tourists. As the four approach the raft, one of the boys notices a black shape in the water. By the time the last swimmer is safely on the raft, the shape is right below them. One by one it devours them. King describes their deaths in clear, graphic, almost loving prose. But he never defines what the black thing is. It is horror incarnate, coming from nowhere to destroy, and that is what makes the story so chilling.

In Cycle of the Werewolf, King narrates a horror that cannot be explained; to do so would rob it of most of its power. A werewolf has come to Tarker's Mills, but there is no reason for its presence, just as there is no reason for Barlow's existence in 'Salem's Lot, or the Overlook's malevolence in The Shining, or the Dark Man in The Stand. "There is no more reason for its coming now," King writes, "than there would be for the arrival of cancer, or a psychotic with murder on his mind, or a killer tornado. Its time is now, its place is here" (14).

The same is true in <u>Roadwork</u>. There is no reason why Charlie should develop the cancer and die. There is literally no reason why the freeway spur must be built, destroying Dawes´ home and the Blue Ribbon Laundry in the process. The Epilogue bluntly states that the city built the extension simply to avoid losing federal money. This particular "cancer," which destroys Dawes and all that he loves, is superfluous. The image of cancer is particularly important in <u>Roadwork</u>, however, since King works here without the aid of external horror. To make Dawes´ life and death interesting and meaningful, he needs a powerful symbol. Cancer provides that symbol.

One of the most critical episodes in the novel occurs late in the narrative, after Dawes´ wife has left him, after he has had a quick, almost still-born affair with a young hitchhiker, after he has tried to destroy the construction equipment scheduled to level his home. The city has sent him the latest in a series of letters about his situation. It is now December 26, 1973; he must be out of his house by January 19, 1974 or violate the law.

That evening, he remembers his son´s death, how he and Mary first heard about Charlie´s cancer. The dialogue is well handled: Dawes and his wife stunned and disbelieving, the doctor compassionate but distanced, uninvolved. Throughout the passage, King returns to the image of the cancer as a "collection of bad cells roughly the size of a walnut" (188). From something that small had come their son´s progression from headaches to double vision, embarrassing episodes of bedwetting, blindness, partial numbness, lapses into nonsense and obscenity, coma, and finally death.

The cancer was inoperable, the doctor assured them. Nothing could be done. Dawes must face something beyond comprehension: "today a walnut, tomorrow the world. The creeping unknown. The incredible dying son. What was there to understand?" (190).

By itself, the episode is powerful. King

carefully delineates the mental anguish of a father facing the death of a son, compounded by Dawes' own insecurities and fears, signaled by his first reaction to the news--"Thank God it's not me" (189). But King has so structured the novel that the episode functions on several levels, each deeper than this superficial one, and each more potent.

On a second level, the episode defines Dawes' fear of cancer, and King's, reaching backward and forward, like a cancer itself, to color everything else in the novel. The casual references to people dying of cancer earlier in the book reverberate as we see how deeply such references must have wounded Dawes. Subsequent references no longer pretend to be casual, dispassionate bits of data. Each reference recalls Charlie's death, the psychic wound that has incapacitated Dawes and forced him into the role of a Nick Adams struggling against disintegration.

The episode illustrates the underlying theme of <u>Roadwork</u>, simultaneously defining ambiguities implicit in the title itself. Dawes refers to his discovery that "God had decided to do a little roadwork on their son Charlie's brain" (187). Cancer and roadwork become one, images of an inexplicable threat Dawes must somehow overcome but cannot. That single clause ties together much of the novel, explaining plot, characterization, motivation, and resolution. One cancer has destroyed Dawes' son. Another cancer, a social cancer, is destroying Dawes' life. He fights it, but, like Charlie's collection of cells, this cancer is also inoperable. Nothing Dawes can do will save his home, his marriage, his livelihood, everything he holds important. A cancer eats away at him until he systematically reduces his options to one: death. His own cancer is as devastating as Charlie's was.

For Dawes, life is indeed a "shaky ceasefire," to borrow the phrase from the beginning and the conclusion of <u>Roadwork</u>. Like Nick Adams, Dawes simply tries to keep things from flying apart. Adams succeeds by re-creating the ritual of fishing; Dawes hopes to succeed by preserving the rituals of his life: his home, the room where Charlie died, the attic where the boy's clothing is stored. Mary reacted externally to Charlie's death by crying, drinking, and mourning. Then she emerged from her loss. Dawes' scars are internal, harder to see and longer in healing.

When the still festering wound of Charlie's death merges with the new cancer, the encroaching roadwork, Dawes simply cannot accept reality.

His situation leads directly and logically to a secondary theme in Roadwork, King's critique of the family. As happens frequently in King's fiction, families fail. Dawes' situation is more extreme than that of many of King's characters. The fundamental family unit of father, mother, single child has already been disrupted by death, his family truncated, before the narrative begins.

His first real loss in the novel seems more related to business than to family, but that appearance is deceptive. For Dawes, the Blue Ribbon Laundry is family. His first recollections in the novel are not of his dead son, but of his employers. They are also dead, as is the way of business they encouraged. Dawes is crippled by the new management of the laundry. Steve Ordner cares less about people than about the laundry's status as one of the conglomerate's many investments. Ordner sees the problems Dawes causes as inconveniences, gauging them in terms of his own standing with the company. At the moment of crisis, Ordner and others do not perceive the intensity of Dawes' commitment to the laundry as it was or his disgust with what it has become. He strings them along; they accept his deceptions, unable to believe that any sane man would consciously throw away what Dawes has achieved. Like the principal in Rage, they can handle anything except irrationality.

Without the support the Tarkingtons had given their employees, Dawes is thrown back onto his family. Here again, he meets with failure. Mary withdraws from him, forcing him deeper into his memories. Charlie's death separates them and distances them from memories of earlier, happier times together. Dawes recalls many of those moments, ironic counterpoints to the current state of his marriage.

Mary is concerned from the first about Dawes' attitudes. She knows that they have only a few weeks to find a new home, but he seems in no hurry. She questions him, but does not force him to act. As Steve Ordner had in relocating the laundry, she allows Dawes to deceive her. He tells her about houses he has never looked at; she accepts his stories and hopes that the next house will be better. Later, she is ill with a cold and cannot go out with him. He continues the charade, discussing in detail houses they might yet buy.

Much of her willingness to accept his word seems psychological stasis. She responded to Charlie's death by closing others off, including Dawes. In addition, from her perspective their marriage has gone wrong since Charlie's death. She believes that Dawes is punishing her; her first child miscarried, and Charlie was born with a "built-in self-destruct." She refers to Charlie as "your son," screaming at Dawes and pulling away from his touch. At this point, their separation becomes complete. They stare at each other "as if they had discovered for the first time that there was more to them than they had ever dreamed of--vast white spaces on some interior map" (99). Mary leaves the house, moving in with her parents and resuming the life interrupted by her marriage to Dawes. Each time they meet, she has changed, becoming less what she was as wife and mother, more herself.

Dawes recognizes her increasing independence. What is more, he approves of it. She has regained herself, he realizes, externalizing her loss and adapting to it, just as she had been able to adapt to Charlie's death. Finally, they speak of formalizing their break through divorce. Dawes has lost irrecovably his last remaining link with his ordered past, except for his house.

Charlie--Charles Frederick Dawes--is one of the most important characters in the novel, even though he never appears except in Dawes' memories. He stands for the stability Dawes has lost.

Through Charlie, King brings the image of a cancer to the surface, literalizing what has been symbolic, parallelling Charlie's life to American society in the throes of the energy crisis. Both had seemed healthy, strong, alert, and independent. Both were stricken suddenly by hidden maladies. In Charlie's case, the symptoms seemed unimportant at first, only later revealing the fatal nature of the illness--the walnut-sized tumor in his brain. In the case of the American economy, the same was true. Everywhere Dawes turns, he sees evidence of enormous changes resulting from the energy shortage. He takes malicious pleasure in driving above the fifty-five limit, wasting gasoline and flaunting conservationists he passes. In a fit of anger, he turns on every appliance in the house, rebelling not so much against saving energy as against the Pavlovian conditioning he sees everywhere. Dawes' meetings with Drake, a former minister, at the Drop Down Mama Coffeehouse allows him to see the first victims of the altered American social consciousness, the vagrants and misfits who (like Ben Richards and his family in The Running Man) have no real hope of surviving. The world he knows is changing beyond his ability to adapt, and he takes recourse in insanity. One of the devastating ironies of Roadwork is that Dawes dies to prevent an unnecessary freeway extension from being built. Construction proceeds in spite of him, yet after 1974, there would be even less need for highways in general as American driving habits changed (at least temporarily).

All of this seems to put a heavy burden on poor Charlie, yet the symbolic parallels seem inherent in the text. In addition, Charlie is present far more than one might otherwise note. From first page to last, Dawes carries on a dialogue with "Freddy," his name for the irrational self within. Initially, the dialogue is confusing, since "Freddy" has no identity in the context of the narrative. Midway through Roadwork, however, King provides several necessary clues. Dawes watches television--old programs, game shows, Saturday morning adventures. Mary asks him why. He answers that he wants to talk with his kids about things--but he has no kids. The first miscarried and Charlie is dead. At that point, Dawes gives Charlie's full name: Charles Frederick Dawes. Charlie and Freddy are "reunited by the wonders of the subconscious mind" (105).

In a sense, then, Dawes is both himself and his dead son. He dreams continually of Charlie and of killing him through negligence or an inability to act. On one level, of course, the dreams are accurate. Once the cancer had been diagnosed, there was nothing Dawes could do. On another, however, the dreams become Dawes' own cancer. He becomes obsessed with Charlie, with his loss, with the tragic unfairness of Charlie's death. To that extent, he becomes Charlie. He cannot disengage himself from his dreams and his memories, and ultimately that engagement destroys him.

With Charlie dead and Mary gone, Dawes becomes isolated. He sees few of his old friends; their meetings are brief and painful. He meets a former employee and tries to warn him about the conglomerate mentality of his employers; the man smashes Dawes in the face and leaves. Dawes picks up a hitch-hiker one evening. She spends the night at his home. In spite of his initial protests, he sleeps with her. She restores his sense of virility momentarily, but not even that is sufficient to alter his self-destructive course of action. He gives her money, talks with her on the telephone on Christmas Day, but does not allow her to change his purpose. When the city officials threaten to expose his infidelity, Dawes does not care, since his marriage is already finished. In the end, he arranges for the girl to receive enough money to begin her life over again, even though he is convinced that there are no new beginnings . . . just the same circles repeating endlessly.

His only point of contact, ironically, is with an individual even more isolated than Dawes himself. Salvatore Maglione, dealer in Cadillacs no one wants to buy and illicit commodities Dawes is desperate to buy, gives Dawes his final chance for human contact. Curiously, the two establish a grudging mutual respect, each recognizing the other's commitment to individual values. While those values may not be shared by society as a whole, they do give form and meaning to Maglione's life, something Dawes respects.

Finally, though, even that brief alliance is broken, and Dawes is totally alone. Just him, his house, and his memories.

The climax of <u>Roadwork</u> succeeds less because of any inherent suspense than because of King's careful creation of mental states. Dawes cannot win; that has been clear from the beginning. When he destroyed the construction equipment, he had set the project back a month or two, nothing more. The highway, like Charlie's cancer, cannot be stopped. Nor can he bend to accommodate to change. He has already excised himself from any lasting relationships: wife, friends, business. He refuses to re-integrate himself into that world, cutting Olivia out even as she tries to save him. In his death, he again recalls Nick Adams, and perhaps Hemingway himself. When one can no longer accept what life offers, one bows out with whatever grace is possible. In Dawes's case, that requires a certain degree of violence, self-directed and largely self-inflicted. The last page of the novel (excluding the Epilogue) neatly completes the references to Nick Adams and the Hemingway mystique. Dawes says good-bye to Nick Adams, touches the alligator clip to the battery terminal, and closes his eyes. His final thoughts are that the explosion seems about the size of a walnut.

<u>Roadwork</u> is more intricately plotted than either <u>Rage</u> or <u>The Long Walk</u>, more on a par with the works published under King's own name. In addition, it is self-reflexive, a novel in part about people creating fictions. The metaphor of God as novelist occurs at a critical point in the narrative, just after Dawes speaks to Olivia about his "soul-cancer." She accuses him of egotism; he responds by saying that things will turn out as they must. The only thing that bothers him, he

continues, is an intermittent sense that he is a "character in some bad writer's book and he's already decided how things are going to turn out and why." It's easier that way, he concludes. The bad writer includes his son's cancer as chapter one; suicide or no suicide fills out the last chapter, just before the epilogue. "It's a stupid story," he concludes (181).

It is also the story of <u>Roadwork</u>. King writes his own synopsis, his own ironic evaluation of a frighteningly realistic narrative about a man who cannot swim against the current, to return for a moment to "Big Two-Hearted River." It is pessimistic, as <u>Rage</u>, <u>The Long Walk</u> and <u>The Running Man</u> might be considered pessimistic. Characters sacrifice themselves, but nothing really changes. Only the individual's integrity, however distorted it might be, remains to give meaning to death.

<u>Roadwork</u> is also complex in its attitude toward literature and generic definition. Like <u>Rage</u> and <u>The Long Walk</u>, it is primarily a mainstream novel. There is no supernatural horror, little science fiction; what horror it generates is more psychological than anything. Yet like the first two Bachman novels, it constantly alludes to other genres as motifs. In the early pages, King refers to science fiction. A commercial from Exxon about the energy crisis suggests a science fiction crisis much like the one King wrote about in "Star Invaders," an early self-published story (46-47); the energy shortage is a science fiction crisis (68). A national news broadcast closes by announcing that flying saucers had been spotted in Ohio (78). Later Dawes falls asleep while watching John Agar in <u>Brain From Planet Arous</u> (125).

From that point on, however, references to science fiction disappear, as if King wants to alert the reader that rational, technological solutions have become invalid. Instead, the text refers to horror. A restaurant becomes "horribly" quiet (144); a letter from <u>them</u> (the city authorities) reminds him of a horror movie poster (185); episodes remind him of Poe, of Lovecraft. A doctor treating a stricken woman in a Shop'n'Save

89

looks as if he had "just realized that his profession would dog him to his grave, like some vengeful horror monster" (214). The novel avoids horror, yet even in avoiding manages to assert it.

The self-reflexive references to science fiction and horror fulfill larger purposes in the novel, however, beyond merely creating an atmosphere or suggesting a narrative movement. Allusions to science fiction, particularly in the context of social criticism, prepare for The Running Man, the next Bachman novel and the one most clearly allied to science fiction. The references to horror similarly establish connections with other works published under King's own name.

Although such analyses are now at best academic, there are a number of passages in Roadwork that create imagistic connections between the novel and King's other fictions. Salvatore Maglione has counterparts in mafioso types in Thinner and short stories such as "The Man With a Belly," "Battleground," and "The Wedding Gig." Dawes' lighthearted comment about Mary becoming a prostitute (57) foreshadows a similar but more serious situation in The Running Man. Dawes' obsession with game shows looks both backward and forward, to The Long Walk and The Running Man. A Kafkaesque dream in which Dawes kills himself by putting an aerosol can in his mouth and inhaling until he balloons suggests "The Blue Air Compressor." The presence of a laundry, specifically the Blue Ribbon Laundry, establishes connections with Rage and Carrie, as well as stories such as "The Mangler," "Big Wheels: A Story of the Laundry Game," and others that touch upon that portion of King's own biography.

All of this is to say that Roadwork seems ambivalent. More clearly a psychological, mainstream novel than any of his major works, it also bears the marks of King's craftsmanship. It is the novel least like any of his others, yet even in that dissimilarity, it allows him to explore familiar territory. By approaching that territory from a new direction, he gives his readers unusual and interesting perspectives, well worth the effort of discovering.

By the end Roadwork, he even seems to have answered the initial question: Why does the novel begin with "But," the second half of an undefined opposition. By 1974, he seems to say, the nation might have begun recovering collectively from the trauma of Vietnam, a divisiveness he had illustrated graphically in his "Garbage Truck" column for May 15, 1969 as he narrated the events surrounding a Peace March at the University of Maine. Collectively, we may recover; but, as he demonstrates so persuasively in virtually everything he has written, it is not that easy for individuals to excise their own private cancers.

Chapter VI

THE RUNNING MAN

The appearance of *The Running Man* in 1982 marked the last of the non-horror novels King published as Richard Bachman. The fifth Bachman novel, *Thinner*, would turn explicitly to horror, using style, plot, and content so archetypally King's that readers would assert his authorship long before he publicly acknowledged it.

In addition, it may be the last of the Bachman novels to draw explicitly on King's college experiences. *Thinner* seems much closer to *The Talisman* than to *Carrie*, more a product of the mature King. *The Running Man*, on the other hand, carries to its logical conclusion an idea King toyed with in "Garbage Truck," his weekly column for *The Maine Campus*. In March of 1969, King devoted a column to the "new trend in entertainment--the cheapie game show," noting the lack of shows for watchers over thirty. His suggestion? A series of new shows, including *The Middle-Aged Game*, hosted by Bud Collyer; *The Brutality Game*, hosted by Dick Daley, pitting contestants against forty Chicago policemen; *The Divorce Game*, hosted by Zsa Zsa Gabor, ending with the losing couples stoning each other; *The Wife-Swapping Game*, with Ann Landers and Dr. Joyce Brothers; and *The Burial Game* with Vincent Price, the winner to receive a lifetime membership in the American Mortician's Association and "a free fill-up when he finally lands on the embalming slab" (9). The column was openly, bitingly satirical. In its own way, so is *The Running Man*, based on a future game show in which losing contestants die--and no one has ever won.

In another way, however, *The Running Man* seems anomalous, even among the non-horror Bachman novels. It is the first to exploit fully the possibilities of yet another genre, science fiction.

Rage and Roadwork are primarily mainstream, psychological suspense novels, containing few elements other than style or diction to connect them with science fiction or horror. Plot, characterization, and setting all define a world like our own. The Long Walk is less direct. Its setting suggests a future, alternative society, but King does not develop that society beyond subtle hints and half-veiled allusions. The novel is not about any possible future society as much as it is about Ray Garraty and the other Walkers. To that degree, the novel uses science fiction only as a background against which to delineate contemporary characters and explore social relationships.

The Running Man, on the other hand, is explicitly science fiction, the only one of King's novels to depend heavily upon a popular genre other than horror.

It is one thing to call a novel "science fiction," of course, and quite another to demonstrate how and why it should be so classified. "Science fiction" is itself a difficult phrase to define. Almost every practitioner has contributed a definition to the pool, without any arriving at an acceptable consensus. Damon Knight discusses a number of definitions, from Brian W. Aldiss' "search for a definition of man and his status in the universe which will stand in our advanced but confused state of knowledge (science), and . . . characteristically cast in the Gothic or post-Gothic mode" to Norman Spinrad's "Science fiction is anything published as science fiction" (62-63). Knight developed a list of characteristics common to most definitions of "science fiction":

* Science is basic to the fictional society and its assumptions about humanity;

* Technology and invention are presented as common and expected;

* The writer has access to humanity's past, present, and future, including time-travel;

* The narratives extrapolate from present to

possible (or even probable) futures, without any overt sense of prediction;

* The scientific method is a basic mode of knowing in the fictions;

* Settings allow for distant planets, other dimensions, etc.;

* And the plots include catastrophes, either natural or man-made (63).

In general, science fiction explores the effects of technology or science on human communities, often by extrapolating from present situations to future ones, those changes frequently threatening a catastrophe of culture-wide, often planet-wide or galaxy-wide proportions.

This digression into definition is important in discussing The Running Man, since here, for the first and perhaps only time, King attempts a fully realized, novel-length portrayal of a science fictional world. In spite of the predominance of horror fantasy in his canon, King has worked briefly with science fiction. One of his earliest was "The Star Invaders" (1964). The narrative is at times rough, the characterization trite and stereotypic, understandable in a seventeen-year-old author who would not publish a story professionally until 1965. Still, it demonstrates a thorough knowledge of the conventions associated with a genre King had already read and enjoyed for almost a decade.

His interest in science fiction, while subordinate to his interest in horror fantasy, continues. "I Am The Doorway" (1971) is a story about aliens possessing a human body. "Night Surf" (1974) is as much extrapolative science fiction as an evocation of horror and a precursor to the "superflu" in The Stand. "Beachworld" (1985) is also explicitly science fiction, looking at alien worlds and alien life-forms as it moves gradually into supernatural (or at least extra-terrestrial) horror.

Any precise differentiation between science

fiction and horror fantasy is largely irrelevant in discussing King's work, however, for two reasons. First, King himself is not particularly interested in a finely drawn distinction. It is, he says in Danse Macabre, a boring academic subject on a par with discussions of how many angels can dance on the head of a pin. Fantasy and science fiction are both works of the imagination, he continues, and both "try to create worlds which do not exist, cannot exist, or do not exist yet" (29).

Second, and more critical, King's own works suggest an unusually fluid border between science fiction and fantasy. "I Am The Doorway" certainly has its share of horror motifs, of inexplicable monsters and delicious terrors. "Night Surf" is more atmospheric than scientific, with "Captain Trips" more evocative than rigidly scientific. The Stand illustrates King's ability to shift from one genre to another within a single novel. It begins as a SF disaster novel, with science and technology, extrapolation, the near future, and a man-made catastrophe. But it shifts genres as characters establish a new equilibrium in a new world. Even as they re-create the human community, the characters move into fantasy, where dreams come true and a Dark Man waits out West to destroy all things good.

"Beachworld" is similar. The opening pages are science fiction: a space ship crashes on an alien world covered with sand dunes. The survivors communicate with a rescue vessel. The vessel arrives and tries to rescue both survivors. At that point, however, King shifts again. The sand is sentient; perhaps the planet itself is a sentient creature, as in Stanislaw Lem's Solaris, with its ocean entity. The conclusion of the story becomes as much horror as science fiction. The "monster" is impossible but exists nonetheless.

To read The Running Man, then, is to receive a new sense of King's interest in science fiction as a separate genre and to see how he infuses even a straight-forward SF narrative with a sense of the horrific.

There is little doubt that the novel begins as science fiction. Samuel R. Delany has defined what he calls the "protocols" of science fiction. The genre, he argues, requires that readers come to texts with different assumptions than they would use for mainstream fiction. Those assumpions control the way the reader interprets the text and are in turn developed through the text, particularly through language.

The opening paragraphs of The Running Man create a different tone than the opening lines of, say, Cujo, published the year before. "Once upon a time," Cujo begins, evoking the age-old convention of the fairy tale; it then undercuts that same convention as it continues, "not so long ago, a monster came to the small town of Castle Rock, Maine." In spite of the realism that Winter finds in Cujo, King explicitly relates it to one of the most traditional forms of the fantastic. In this world, the novel argues, fairy tales may be quite unpleasant.

The Running Man, on the other hand, does not belong to "this" world at all. The word choice and imagery of the opening pages separate the novel from contemporary American society; it is an extreme reflection of it, perhaps, but does not represent that society directly.

The first words a reader encounters, the chapter heading, immediately suggests space travel and technology:

. . . Minus 100
and COUNTING . . .

The "countdown" continues throughout the novel, an implacable reminder of genre and form. King uses the formula carefully, modulating the reader's sense of time and duration. The closing pages seem to rush by, as the formula is repeated more frequently, the countdown numbers breaking into the narrative more rapidly: 005, 004, 003, 002, 001. At that point, there is both ignition and lift-off and the novel reaches its logical, inexorable climax. The final chapter heading, "000," indicates both the conclusion of the narrative and the state the society represented has achieved.

On another level, however, the "countdown" formula simultaneously insists that the novel engages the author's concern for technological change, epitomized by but not restricted to space flight. This secondary sense receives added impetus as the novel works through the opening paragraphs, confronting the reader with a number of initially unidentified characteristics of this future society. We read of "Co-Op City," a place that does not yet exist, while the name suggests its nature. That suggestion is amplified by phrases creating imagistic analogues between the city and a slum-prison through details such as "ragged wash" on clotheslines and "rats and plump alley cats" living in the garbage. The adjective "plump" itself creates an image of this new world.

We read about "Free-Vee," a phrase that defines itself by blending TV with King's emerging image of a futuristic welfare state. Legislation has mandated Free-Vee in every "Development apartment," King notes, but the "Compulsory Benefit Law of 2021" had not passed, allowing people the marginal freedom to turn the Free-Vee off. When King interrupts his narrative briefly to discuss Free-Vee programming, he confirms the reader's sense of a dystopian future and introduces a key motif. The main character, Ben Richards, normally does not watch Free-Vee. But his infant daughter is desperately ill and he cannot find work, forcing him to rely on what his wife Sheila can earn "on her back." Recently, however, he has begun watching Free-Vee intently, particularly high-stakes game show like <u>Treadmill to Bucks</u>, in which chronically ill patients receive money for answering questions while working out on a treadmill. Failure on a question means a deduction of winnings and a faster treadmill. Eventually, since the show restricts contestants to those with serious heart, liver, or lung disease, many of the participants die on screen, providing the audience with the ultimate game-show thrill. As King had noted in <u>The Long Walk</u>, "The Ultimate Game show would be one where a losing contestant was killed" (Ch. 4).

In the world of The Running Man, that is precisely the case. King has taken a hint from science fiction and gone beyond his satirical observations in "Garbage Truck" to create a future society controlled by the Network, which in turn depends upon game shows for its continued popularity . . . and for controlling the masses. The names of the shows define their content and suggest the world in which King has placed us. In addition to Treadmill to Bucks, Free-Vee offers Fun Guns, Dig Your Grave, How Hot Can You Take It, Swim the Crocodiles, Run For Your Guns, and, of course, the central game, The Running Man. King's title defines not only Richards' actions but the format for the best-paying game show on Free-Vee.

On The Running Man, carefully screened contestants are introduced to the Free-Vee audience while the emcee works the studio audience up to a fever of hatred toward the contestant, who then leaves the studio. He has twelve hours of grace and a stake of $4,800 "running money"; at the end of four days, he receives an additional hundred dollars an hour for every hour he remains alive. Concerned citizens reporting his presence receive a hundred dollar reward; a sighting that leads to a kill earns the citizen $1,000. Amateur photographers can earn ten dollars per foot for film of the Runners. The Runners must mail in two film packets per day; failure to do so makes them ineligible to win the prize . . . but the Hunt continues nonetheless. The packets, of course, form the nucleus for the day's prime-time Free-Vee show. In addition, the Network has its own team of hunters, headed by the infamous Evan McCone. If the Runner survives for thirty days, he receives a reward of $1,000,000,000, which parallels The Prize in The Long Walk in two critical ways: first, it represents more wealth than any contestant can imagine; and second, no one has ever collected it. When Richards begins his run, the record stands at eight days.

The Running Man follows the pattern of allusion King developed in the first three Bachman novels, but understandably mutes that pattern. Since it concerns a future society in which reading has virtually disappeared, it refers less frequently to literary sources. There is a single reference to Shakespeare, in the form of a quotation from Lady Macbeth immediately after she murders Duncan (211); one to Lewis Carroll's "The Walrus and the Carpenter" (202); one to Robert Frost's "The Road Not Taken," an ironically apt poem in view of the emphasis on movement and choice in the novel; and one that looks obliquely at both the Hemingway mystique and King's use of it in Roadwork: Richards "understood well enough how a man with a choice between pride and responsibility will almost always choose pride--if responsibility robs him of his manhood" (106). Dawes has no responsibilities left and can follow his pride; Ben Richard submits to the indignity of being The Running Man as the only way to support his family.

The novel also mentions two central figures in science fiction and dystopian literature, H. G. Wells and George Orwell. The Wells references remind readers of what science fiction traditionally entails. In one instance, Richards has arrived at Voigt Airfield just before his final confrontation with the Network. As Richards enters the airfield, King describes the control tower as resembling an H. G. Wells Martian. The image is similar to those in The Long Walk and Roadwork in which King describes power lines or construction equipment as mantidae; the reader imagines a human artifact in visual, metaphorical terms. The difference, of course, is that the earlier novels depend upon images King frequently associates with the insectile creatures of 1950's horror films; the later novel borrows from Wells, one of the fathers of science fiction. And while Wells' Martians certainly expressed more than a modicum of horror, they remain essentially science fictional, that is, knowable through scientific methodology.

The second reference to Wells operates on much the same level. Late in the novel, as Richards flies southward toward Network headquarters, he imagines missile silos opening like gateways to the subterranean world of Morlocks

(189). The allusion to *The Time Machine* is again appropriate for *The Running Man*. In a sense, King has provided a time machine of his own, transporting the reader forward to twenty-first century America. His extrapolated society likewise divides into two distinct categories. Earlier, as Richards had driven through a crowd, he noted that the spectators lined up along the street. On one side were the upper- and middle-class citizens, the Eloi of this new world, spotless and well-coiffured. Richards has taken one of them hostage, Amelia Williams; he has commandeered her car and forced her to drive him to Voigt Field. In doing so, he has intruded an ugly reality into her otherwise idealized life, just as the intrusion of the Morlocks disrupts the Eloi's lives in Wells' fable. And, again like the Eloi, King's citizens seem vaguely incomplete, "like pictures with holes for eyes or a jigsaw puzzle with a minor piece missing" (152). What is missing is desperation.

On the other side of the street are Richards' own people, the Morlock analogues who live in darkness and filth and disease, laboring to support the leisure classes. They work in deadly conditions; Richards is sterile from his years working in a badly shielded General Atomics nuclear plant. They breathe polluted air, even though GA could produce effective nose filters for pennies but chooses (presumably for political as well as economic reasons) not to. Again, King's description suggests Wells' second great division of humanity: "Red noses with burst veins. Flattened, sagging breasts. Stringy hair. White socks. Cold sores. Pimples. The blank and hanging mouths of idiocy" (153). As in *The Time Machine*, humanity has bifurcated, a situation engendered and sustained by the Network.

The novel also looks at Orwell's *1984*. In the second chapter, Richards approaches the Network Building, a skyscraper that, like Orwell's pyramidal Ministry of Love (ironically nicknamed "Miniluv"), overshadows the landscape, rivetting all eyes upon its imposing, threatening bulk. Halfway through the novel, Richards goes to the public library to read what he can about air pollution. He finds little written after 2002, and what he finds does not correspond with what had been written earlier. The government, he notes, was doing its "tardy but efficient job of double thinking" (105). The world of The Running Man is as inimical to individuality as was Orwell's imaginary society in 1984. Big Brother almost literally watches over Richards' shoulder throughout; by submitting the two film packets daily, Richards contributes to the sense that "They" know his every move.

Several additional influences seem critical in The Running Man, although in these cases King refers less to specific quotations than to general themes. The first is Frederik Pohl and C. M. Kornbluth's brilliant extrapolative satire of a world governed by Big Business, The Space Merchants (1953)[1]. In the world of The Space Merchants, advertising has become paramount. Comsumers are important because they consume; any manipulative techniques that increase consumption are considered ethical and proper, regardless of their impact on the consumers. The novel is at times comic, at times virulently caustic as Pohl and Kornbluth describe logical outgrowths of trends they perceived in the early 1950's.

In its own way, and for its own purposes, The Running Man parallels The Space Merchants. It replaces advertising with the media, specifically with television as manipulative arm for a government controlled by, and at times supplanted by, the Network. The Network not only organizes and televises the various games, but issues its own legal bills of execution. General Atomics is an equal force in the government, keeping workers in conditions that result in deformity, sterility, and death, all with the tacit or explicit approval of whatever governmental forms still exist.

Even more directly, The Running Man owes much to Ray Bradbury and Fahrenheit 451 (1953).[2] Free-Vee seems a direct descendant of Bradbury's wall-sized televisions; their pervasiveness in the society described equally so. For most of the people in The Running Man, Free-Vee substitutes for thought, for life, for engagement with others on any meaningful level. King implicitly rejects Free-Vee in the opening pages of the novel, as he comments that neither Benjamin Richards nor his wife watched Free-Vee; when Richards begins to watch the game shows avidly, Sheila knows that something is desperately wrong. Once Richards appears on the screen, it becomes clear that television has replaced rational thought. Viewers respond emotionally to lies and contradictions, never questioning what comes over the Free-Vee sets. This unthinking acceptance of media manipulation is at first Richard's greatest difficulty; then, once he understands and accepts the full influence of Free-Vee on political realities, he reverses the procedure and manipulates the media to its own destruction.

Like Bradbury's world in <u>Fahrenheit 451</u>, King's world in <u>The Running Man</u> is aliterate. When Richards is sequestered prior to his appearance on the game show, he asks for something to read. The guard reacts with surprise. Richards must explain what he wants: novels, thick books with stories. The guard returns with three volumes, apparently chosen more for thickness than content. Richards' world exists largely without the printed page; by default, Free-Vee has moved in, altering reality to suit its own needs. People speak and think in visual, rather than verbal images.

A third influence is Loren Singer's <u>The Parallax View</u> (1970). King has mentioned this novel several times in interviews; Winter names it in <u>The Art of Darkness</u> in reference to King's first attempt to place a novel with Doubleday. Just after completing "Getting It On" in 1970, Winter says, King borrowed Singer's novel from the Bangor Public Library. Noting a number of similarities between what Singer had accomplished and what he had attempted, King sent a letter about his manuscript to Doubleday, addressed to "The Editor of <u>The Parallax View</u>." That editor was unavailable and the manuscript was forwarded to Bill Thompson, who later accepted <u>Carrie</u> for Doubleday (25).

Reading the Bachman novels (or even King's novels under his own name) and then going to The Parallax View, however, reveals an interesting situation. The resemblance to Rage, the final published version of "Getting It On," seems faint, depending on the psychological state of protagonists helpless to extricate themselves or others from traps imposed by society. Both novels conclude with the defeat of the central character; Charlie Decker is committed indefinitely, and Malcolm Graham is murdered by the secret government agency he is trying to expose.

The connections between The Parallax View and The Running Man seem much stronger, however. In both, the authors use the surface narrative of an individual being hunted by government agents to construct a more complex, more meaningful investigation of privacy, freedom, and individual dignity. In both instances, the characters do not fully understand the magnitude of the force they must confront. And midway through each, the characters stop, turn around, and take an offensive that leads to their own deaths, deaths which in the context of the novel punctuate the meaninglessness of the characters' lives. Both novels parallel the character's physical movements through the landscape to their psychological movement from marginal innocence to unwelcome experience. Both men must murder to survive. Both entangle a woman and a child in the web of their own actions; and in both cases that entanglement leads to death. Ultimately, neither is able to penetrate to the center of the hidden force they oppose; each must be content with a marginal victory, although Richards' is more satisfying for the reader.

There is one more novel that influenced The Running Man, King's The Long Walk. Even the names suggest a similarity; in each case, the structure of the novel, as defined by the title, parallels its themes. Ray Garraty's walk becomes an image of life itself; Richards' run symbolizes the helplessness of the individual in a society strangled by the media. Beyond that initial similarity, however, there are a number of intriguing parallels and reversals.

Initially, the two novels are related by genre; both are in some senses science fiction. Both take place in a future America in which government has become more concerned about its own security than its citizens. In both, government forces and police agencies are seen as dangerous rather than as protectors. In both, surface narrative extrapolates from a current state to logical and distasteful extremes. Lotteries play an important role in each, as contestants are selected to participate in games essential to the stability of the economy and the state; in <u>The Long Walk</u>, it is a literal lottery, while in <u>The Running Man</u>, it is a figurative lottery based on circumstances in life. In both, however, the characters become inordinately aware of each passing moment . . . one more moment of life. In each, the crowds of spectators mentally divorce themselves from the contestants, while the crowds' attitudes range from barely disguised blood-lust to overtly sexual stimulation.

There are also a number of significant differences, however, the most important being that <u>The Running Man</u> asserts itself as science fiction on every level, while <u>The Long Walk</u> assumes the structure and setting of science fiction but asserts itself more as horror than as science fiction. <u>The Long Walk</u> does not depend upon any important technological change, nor on the effects of such a change on human society. Perhaps the only technological innovations in the novel are devices that allow the guards to monitor the speed and position of each Walker individually. In <u>The Running Man</u>, on the other hand, technology is central to every episode in the novel. Free-Vee, portable video packs, air cars, unique plastic explosives, instantaneous television sending and receiving on board the escape jet--all are critical to the plot.

They also make more understandable a second major difference, one again symbolized in the two titles. The earlier novel moves at a walk, literally and figuratively. There is virtually no plot; boys walk and talk until they die. In the later novel, Richards runs, again both literally and figuratively . . . again, until he dies. The routes each takes are almost mirror images of each other. At times, Ben Richards passes through the same towns northward that Ray Garraty passed through walking south. The sense of opposition even includes several fundamental reversals in the two novels. In <u>The Long Walk</u>, the point of the game is to determine the winner; in <u>The Running Man</u> the point is that there are no winners, at least not from Richards´ social class. From the beginning, he is identified as a loser. His participation in the game in the first place defines that point, as does the fact that he cannot find a job and must rely on the money his wife makes prostituting herself. In <u>The Long Walk</u>, children die as adults watch; in <u>The Running Man</u>, adults die as children watch. The earlier novel is static; the later explodes with violence and energy. Even the seasons emphasize the oppositions between the two. <u>The Long Walk</u> begins on May Day; <u>The Running Man</u>, as befits its thematic concerns for a society already destroying itself, takes place in the fall. The luxuriously green trees that lined the highway for Ray Garraty are sunbursts of color for Ben Richards; they have not yet been murdered by the pollution from Portland, Manchester, or Boston.

Taken together, the suggestions of other writers and other books (including King´s) give <u>The Running Man</u> an unusual texture. While it avoids being overly derivative, it can call upon the strength of Orwell´s setting, or Wells´ indictment of a divided humanity, or Bradbury´s dystopian vision of a world without books, adding their power to its own.

And it is a powerful novel. Like many of King´s works, it suffers from occasional lapses in style, flirting with vulgarity, for example, when such diction is not necessary. And it becomes overly graphic as King describes a wounded Richards´ attempts to pilot the plane, his hanging intestines catching on various obstacles in the cabin, reminding perhaps too directly of Olson in <u>The Long Walk</u>.

At the same time, however, King seems to be working through one of the major criticisms of his prose, turning literary style into content in a way unusual for him.

King enjoys concrete, visual images. In part, this leads to his "brand name" technique as he ties his imagined worlds to the world we know by having characters eat Campbell's soup or munch on Twinkies or (as in Cujo, The Talisman, and elsewhere) live on nothing but Big Macs. It also accounts for the film-like quality of many of his stories . . . and for the fact that almost all of his novels and several short stories have been, are being, or will be translated into film. In some instances (Children of the Corn, for example), the films do not remain true to his visual images, and they suffer for it. In others, Carrie or "The Ledge" segment of Cat's Eye, the strength of King's imagination lends the films even greater strength.

Another manifestation of this joy in the concrete, however, results in what Paul Gray has called "postliterate prose." In his review of Different Seasons, Gray argues that the stories will frighten only one sort of reader, the "old fashioned book lover" who enjoys language as symbol. In King's novels, Gray continues, language is used "the same way the baseball fan seated behind the hometeam dugout uses placards: to remind those present of what they have already seen." As examples, Gray notes Todd Bowden's initial reaction to meeting Kurt Dussander; the old Nazi didn't sound at all like Colonel Klink from Hogan's Heroes, Todd's imagistic model of what Nazis were and did. His imagination, like that of other characters in Different Seasons, "short-circuit[s] thought, plugging directly into prefabricated images." Dick Bowden is described as looking like Lloyd Bochner, a well-known character actor. In "The Body," Gordon Lachance provides his own mood music by imagining "scary violin music" at the appropriate time. Again and again, Gray insists, King falls back on imagery drawn from television or film or comic books or cartoons.

Gray's analysis is generally even-handed, but there is no missing his disapproval of the technique, in spite of his mentioning Thomas Pynchon and Donald Barthelme as other writers who have "toyed . . . with the mass-produced icons that have invaded the communal memory." For such writers, and particularly for King, Gray concludes, "reality is at its most intense when it can be expressed as an animated drawing."

Gray is correct in his assessment and in his definition of King's techniques. He even comes close to providing some psychological justification for the techniques when he refers to King as a "devoted child of the audiovisual age" who writes to the accompaniment of Rock 'n' Roll music.

Gray's criticisms are perhaps germane to some of King's narratives. References in his novels and stories to films, cartoons, and even Rock 'n' Roll occasionally seem digressive. But in The Running Man King's style finds its ideal counterpoint in the content. Here, the language of the novel is decidedly and possibly consciously "postliterate." In one scene, Richards envisions life as a twenty-four-hour television channel, where the "national anthem never plays before sign-off" (141). In another, Richards tries to project into his voice the sincerity and threat he remembered from old television gangster movies (147-148). Later, ties between the media and reality become explicit when Richards first meets Evan McCone, the Network Hunter. He sees McCone as if for the first time, in spite of McCone's frequent exposure on 3-D television. The reality, Richards notes, had taken on a "curious tone of hallucination, as if entity had no right to exist separate from image" (169-170); in the world of The Running Man, image creates reality, not the other way around. The sense of implicit disparity between what one sees and what exists heightens when Richards looks out the window of a jet plane for the first time; he wonders if the landscape below is not merely an illusion generated by media technology: 3-D projectors outside each window and the like. The important point is that Richards thinks in terms of _visual_ media, not printed. The "newsies" (newspapers), King tells us, have long since been killed by Free-Vee.

A second important point is that in spite of his habitually couching his thoughts in patterns ("prefabricated images" to use Gray´s phrase) borrowed from Free-Vee and the visual media, Richards is the closest approximation to a literate man his society can produce. He defines himself as a throwback, a dinosaur; Killian, the Network executive Richards meets, sees him as analogous to cave art or Egyptian urns--a thing to be collected and preserved for its antique value. He holds unpopular attitudes: a man should work at whatever he can to support his family; a man should keep his promises and remain loyal to those who help him. And he reads. In several episodes, Richards holes up in some momentarily safe place and reads. He understands enough about his past to try to discover the truth underlying media propaganda and media images.

To the Network, however, he is an embryonic trouble maker, a potential radical best removed by destroying him in the games, thereby entertaining the viewers and enhancing the Network´s rating. King´s use of science fiction as genre and structural device coalesces with his "post-literate" style. He describes the society in which such a style is absolute, precisely because literary values have disappeared. Virtually no one reads in this world. The information required to build inexpensive nose filters, for example, is available in the public library, but few realize it. A gang of ghetto youths infiltrate the library and bring out the necessary plans, then build their own pollution testers and filters. By doing so, they threaten the control General Atomics and the Network retain over a society in which pollution testers do not officially exist and nose filters cost hundreds of dollars. Richards is not highly literate, but in a nation of blind men, a man with one eye could be king.

King´s style, then, matches his content perfectly; _The Running Man_ becomes not only science fiction but social criticism. A child of the fifties himself, addicted to SF films and Rock 'n' Roll and visual imagery, King incorporates these elements into his prose. In this instance, however the inclusion is fundamental to plot. How he writes is what he describes; Richards' world depends upon the visual at the expense of the verbal.

At the same time that King explores these possibilities of style and content, he also investigates themes and motifs that have recurred throughout the Bachman novels. Central to <u>The Running Man</u>, as to <u>Rage</u>, <u>The Long Walk</u>, and <u>Roadwork</u>, are questions of family and society. Richards is a family man in a sense that Charlie Decker's father, Ray Garraty's father, and Barton George Dawes are not. His nuclear family--father, mother, single child--has not yet been fragmented by hatred, disappearance, or death. Richards knows what his wife must suffer to buy medicine. They know what will happen to their child if they cannot buy more effective medication. Richards' decision to apply for the games is based on his knowledge and his sense of responsibility.

As is also frequent in King's fiction, however, knowledge and a sense of responsibility are insufficient to preserve the family unit. By leaving to apply at the Network, Richards in effect abandons his family. Once he has been accepted, he can communicate only by note; once he becomes a contestant on <u>The Running Man</u>, he is allowed no communication at all with Sheila or Cathy. He has, in effect, isolated them as completely as Garraty's father had . . . or King's own father did.

Beyond that, his actions work against his family. When he sends Sheila Network coupons (the Network prints and distributes its own money, which is preferable even to government script), he removes them from their class, from their own "people," and makes them targets instead of victims. Through a series of circumstances parallelling Vic Trenton's in <u>Cujo</u>, King creates a frightening irony: By trying to protect his family, Ben Richards only succeeds in dooming them.

Mothers also make grave errors. Sheila errs initially by bringing Cathy into a world in which pain and death are endemic. But King shows us little of the Richards' family; Cathy and Sheila disappear after the first few pages, recurring only as Richards remembers them and wonders how they are doing.

Another mother does act in a critical juncture, however, and true to King's patterns in Rage and The Long Walk, her interference is almost fatal. Just as Mrs. Granger and Mrs. Dano destroy children's lives in Rage, or Percy's mother protects him until he is not self-sufficient in The Long Walk, Elton Parrakis' mother destroys him and nearly destroys Richards. Parrakis is one of Richards' contacts; he is to help Richards find a safe hiding place, transmit Richards' daily film packets to a false address, and help him spread the word about the increasing dangers of pollution. Parrakis is overweight, socially inept, and unduly dependent upon his mother. When she discovers who Richards is, she demands that he leave and that Elton dissociate himself from Richards. To make her threat good, she calls the police. As a result, Richards breaks his ankle trying to escape, an injury that makes his death virtually inevitable. Even more critically, Elton is killed. The steering column of his aircar perforates his abdomen, but he lives long enough to deliver Richards to a place of safety and lay a false trail before he dies. Without the interference of Parrakis' inept and hysterical mother, Richards' escape would have been quite different. If Mrs. Parrakis is a monster, she is a monster of insensitivity and lack of understanding.

Other themes show up in The Running Man, often bearing the same weight as in earlier Bachman novels. Sexuality continues as an undercurrent, providing both motivation and threat. The debilitating effects of society on men is symbolized as Richards and other candidates for the games are forced to strip. Many of the men, losers by definition, cannot even afford undergarments. When they stand naked, they become "anonymous, penises dangling between their legs like forgotten war-clubs" (14). They are symbolically impotent, incapable of generating change within their world. Their final recourse is to attempt some change through their own deaths. A few pages later, King emphasizes the sense of impotence as Richards meets a female tester. She is "well-stacked," "tall, Junoesque," dressed in clothing designed to accentuate her femaleness, just as the act of stripping had diminished the men's maleness. Again, sexuality becomes a threat.

Mrs. Parrakis also helps define the threat of sexuality. Her "Eltie," she complains, was a model child until "pooberty"; now he keeps dirty books under his bed and consorts with radical darkies. And when King couples this attitude with his description of the sexual content of the crowd's responses to Richards' actions on the highway and at the airfield, it becomes clear that sexuality in this novel, as in so many of his other works, is potentially (if not actually) destructive.

As a corollary, King also glances at homosexuality, as he has done in each of the preceding Bachman novels. The references are briefer than in <u>Rage</u> or <u>The Long Walk</u>, perhaps because King's character is initially more sure of his own sexual identity than Charlie Decker or Ray Garraty. There are many things he must discover about his world, most of them unpleasant. But he is aware of his own sexuality; after all, he has married and fathered a child in spite of the threatened sterility associated with his job at General Atomics.

But homosexual references occur in the novel and aid in detailing King's extrapolated society. On the one hand, homosexuality is overtly and violently condemned. The first question asked during Richard's medical examination is whether he is homosexual; only afterward is he asked about phobias, use of addictive substances, or treasonable actions against the government (16). A few pages later, Richards refers to a Network "Pal" (slang for man) as "young and slightly faggoty-

looking . . . in a skin-tight Games uniform" (29).
   At the end of the novel, Richards again connects Network personnel with homosexuality. One of the flight crew, the navigator Donahue (later identified as a Network operative), comes back to give Richards a flight map. The man is dressed in tight pants that accentuate his genitalia. Richards' first response is that the man is a "Queer-stomper," one of the wealthy class with leisure to indulge in discriminating violence against homosexuals: "Save our bathroooms for democracy," Richards thinks sarcastically (187). A few scenes later, Donahue threatens Richards, who responds with a counterthreat to blow up the plane. Donahue flinches, then recovers almost immediately. "He might," Richards thinks, "have been promenading on the Cote d'Azur . . . or approaching a gibbering homosexual cowering at the end of a blind alley" (198). About the time everything becomes "very real and in Technicolor" (204) for Richards (note the media-oriented imagery) and he accepts the inevitability of his death, he also notes that from the rear Donahue's buttocks were "as pretty as a girl's" (205). Again, there is the same ambivalence King has shown in the earlier Bachman novels; revulsion battles attraction, with the end result that the characters are continually in a state of disequilibrium. Sexual identity becomes one more great unknown to be faced, even for one who, like Richards, assumes that he knows himself. It is one more potential terror.
   Cancer is another recurring motif in the Bachman novels. In this instance, however, it seems as much functional as symbolic. Richards' world is literally carcinogenic. The air the people breathe destroys their lungs. A five-year-old child is dying from lung cancer that has spread, just as the cancers of pollution and greed are destroying the social body. The cities have become open cancers; the Network, with its assumption of power and its callous treatment of individuals, is a cancer; General Atomics, with its lack of care for its employees' health, is both a cancer and a cause of cancer. In Richards'

112

world, almost everything becomes a cancer, eating at healthy tissue until life itself is threatened. In this novel, King allows the contemporary fear of cancer to develop to its logical extreme, then presents that extreme visually through the figure of a child, screaming in pain as the cancer attacks her body.

In <u>The Running Man</u>, King also approaches several new issues. Most prominent is his overt stand against air pollution. In most of his novels and short stories, people have far too much else to worry about: how to destroy a town full of vampires, or how to escape a rabid dog or malevolent Plymouth Fury. <u>The Running Man</u> represents one of the few times that King becomes almost propagandistic in his attack on a current problem. At times his voice rings stridently, his arguments sincere but overly heavy. The same goes for other social concerns he has infused into the narrative. Ben Richards, the running man, becomes the respository for King´s pronouncements, not only about pollution, but about a society characterized by "limited legal murder, germ warfare in Egypt and South America, and the notorious have-one-kill-one Nevada abortion law" (105). Government by corporation, particularly the Network and General Atomics, comes under attack, as do corporation types, from the lowest flunkies to the executives. But again, the critiques occasionally seem overly strident, out of place in the mouth of a man running for his life.

Still, the novel rivets the reader´s attention on Ben Richards, never digressing for more than seconds at a time. Richards becomes intensely empathetic as, injured and dying, he struggles against the odds--just as Ray Garraty struggled, or Barton George Dawes. The conclusion of Richards´ struggle is as inevitable as were the conclusions to the earlier novels; in the face of such monstrous structures, the individual can hope for little but his own self-respect. Richards´ final action does not destroy the Network; at best it is like Dawes´ attacking construction machinery with homemade Molotov cocktails. The games might be delayed temporarily, but they have not been stopped.

The only change that The Running Man allows for is change within Ben Richards himself. Deprived of everything that humanity requires--home, family, self-respect, pride--he strikes out against the enemy. In his last moments, we barely notice the inherent defeat. He has become, like Hemingway's heroes, his own standard. And his leaving life is as meaningful as his living it.

One of the frequent rumors about King is that he once submitted a science fiction manuscript to DAW Books, only to have it rejected. One variant on the rumor suggests that the novel was simply too bad to be published. In a recent communication, however, King indicated that the novel in question was in fact The Running Man and that it was rejected because DAW was not interested in negative utopias, a reaction, King notes, "which would have left out 1984 and Brave New World, among other things." In addition to putting to rest yet another rumor about "unknown" King novels floating around, his comment also focuses attention on The Running Man. While not as strong as The Long Walk perhaps, or as powerful as The Dead Zone, The Stand, or others of King's novels, it certainly merits more than dismissal as simply another negative utopia.

NOTES

[1] The novel originally appeared in Galaxy Magazine as "Gravy Planet." A subsequent novel, Gladiator-at-Law (1955) similarly satirizes social forms.

[2] Bradbury's novel likewise first appeared in Galaxy Magazine.

Chapter VII

THINNER

Richard Bachman is dead.

In an interview on <u>Good Morning America</u> (12 April 1985), King announced that Bachman had "passed on. He died of cancer of the pseudonym."
That "Richard Bachman" should die in such a way seems appropriate, considering how consistently cancer appears in the Bachman novels. That the cancer should become terminal with <u>Thinner</u> is doubly apt: its characters are obsessed with cancer; and more than the other novels, it seems obviously written by King. Content, style, treatment, tone--all shout "Stephen King."
Even before the publication of <u>Thinner</u>, many readers had wondered about Richard Bachman, but King had denied any connection. Douglas Winter did not even address the issue; the only reference to Bachman in <u>The Art of Darkness</u> occurs in a footnote to <u>The Stand</u> (inaccurately indexed as on page 200, it appears one page later). Winter discusses the central question of <u>The Stand</u>, relating it to Walter Miller´s <u>A Canticle for Leibowitz</u>: Are we doomed to repeat our mistakes throughout history? The question, Winter concludes, may be impossible to resolve. In the accompanying footnote, however, he states that "A recent, unique exploration of this unanswerable question is the dystopian quest novel <u>The Long Walk</u> by Richard Bachman . . . which owes much to Stephen King" (201).
Beyond this single comment, Winter is silent, which drew attention in reviews of <u>The Art of Darkness</u>. One reviewer commented that he had

> only one minor complaint about Doug Winter´s book, which is that it doesn´t offer one piece of information on the

> Richard Bachman-Stephen king [sic] rumor
> that has been floating around for years.
> Well, you can´t win them all. (<u>Fantasy
> Mongers</u>)

Neil Barron´s review of <u>Thinner</u> outlines a number
of parallels between the novel and King´s acknowledged works, then asks:

> Why hasn´t Douglas Winter, whose <u>Stephen
> King: The Art of Darkness</u> . . . is the
> most detailed study of King, discussed
> this? Of course, Winter´s a personal
> friend of King, but more important, he´s
> an attorney, and attorneys don´t reveal
> privileged information, especially if by
> doing so problems with publisher con-
> tracts may result.

For whatever reasons, King denied being
Bachman, while readers argued more insistently
that only he could have written <u>Thinner</u>. Occasionally, comparisons between King and Bachman
must have become almost embarrassing. In one
instance, King is reported to have overheard a
member of the Literary Guild comment that <u>Thinner</u>
was "what Stephen King would write if Stephen King
could really write" ("King´s Too Fast" 26).

In other cases, however, comparisons merely
strengthened the rumors. Mark Graham´s review of
<u>Thinner</u> in December, 1984, presented a case for
King as author:

* <u>Thinner</u> refers to Stephen King in the text.

* <u>Thinner</u> was published by New American
  Library, which published all of King´s
  paperback novels. Even though NAL rarely
  publishes hardcovers, it suddenly published
  a novel by an "unknown New England Writer."

* The novel is set in Maine, as are almost
  all of King´s narratives.

* L.W. Currey had already identified Bachman

as a pseudonym for King.

* And "no one but King could take as off-the-wall a thesis as the one in "Thinner" and make it work." ("Fit For a King")

Given this evidence, Graham says, critics and readers have concluded that Bachman and King are the same individual, and "when you read ´Thinner,´ it is likely you will agree." If the text has not convinced the reader of King´s authorship before the last page, he says, that page will be sufficient. "If King didn´t write the end of this little narrative, his doppelganger did--which of course would be only appropriate."

Barron´s review, published after King´s announcement but written earlier, summarizes Thinner, then suggests that such a plot is insufficient to warrant choice as an alternate selection by the Literary Guild and the Doubleday Book Club; even less sufficient to warrant a first printing of 50,000 copies and an advertising budget of $50,000, particularly when the author had previously published only four paperback novels. When Barron approached Greg Mowry at NAL´s publicity department to request an interview with Bachman, he was told that no interviews were possible but that a letter could be forwarded, with no guarantee of reply.

Barron details all of this, he says, because the extra-literary data supports his contention that King wrote the novel. As additional evidence, Barron notes other connections between King and Bachman, including the importance of laundries in Roadwork, "The Mangler," and King´s own life. Finally, Barron refers to a letter in which King discusses Harper´s rejection of a Bachman novel.

The evidence was clear, it seems, and had been clear for some months: Stephen King was Richard Bachman.

When King acknowledged authorship on February 9, 1985, copies of Thinner disappeared from bookstore shelves within days. Shortly thereafter, copies of the second printing appeared, along with posters and belly-bands proclaiming King´s authorship. Radio stations carried the news. By mid-April, third, fourth, and fifth printings had supplemented the second.

More significantly, Thinner began moving up in the charts. Bestsellers lists for February, March, and April 1985 reveal an intriguing story:

* 10 February: King's announcement was published the day before in the Bangor newspaper; The Talisman is #3 on The New York Times Book Review bestsellers list for the sixteenth week.

* 3 March: The Talisman ranks #4 on the New York Times list, its nineteenth week; Thinner appears at #8.

* 8 March: Within one month of King's announcement, The Talisman is still on the Publishers Weekly list at #5; Thinner appears as #9, with a notation that there are now 230,000 copies in print.

* 17 March: The Los Angeles Times places Thinner at #7, The Talisman at #14.

* 22 March: The Talisman drops to #10 on the Pubishers Weekly list, while Thinner pulls ahead to #7.

* 24 March: The New York Times places Thinner at #4, its fourth week on the list; The Talisman does not appear. (In an interesting irony of circumstance, this issue of Book Review carried a full-page ad for Judy Wardell's Thin Within, promising readers that they can "stay slim forever . . . without dieting," something Billy Halleck might have found in questionable taste.)

* 29 March: Thinner reaches #4 in Publishers Weekly, with The Talisman at #13.

* 7 April: The New York Times lists Thinner

at #3; <u>The Los Angeles Times</u> ranks it #6.

By May 10, <u>Thinner</u> was number one on the <u>Publishers Weekly</u> hardcover bestsellers list.

King's announcement had much to do with the novel's rapid rise, particularly in the month from March 8 to April 5, yet the novel's appearance on bestsellers lists should not be seen as merely a response to that announcement. Certainly many readers would react out of curiosity; the fact that by April paperback copies of the earlier Bachman novels were demanding up to $40.00 at fan conventions indicates that notoriety is certainly playing a large part.

The fact remains, however, that <u>Thinner</u> is itself a strong novel. Even reviewers who concentrated on evidence for King's authorship referred to the novel's intrinsic merits. As the review in <u>Fantasy Mongers</u> asks: "So, what about the book itself? Is it really that good?" The answer the reviewer gives is "an unequivocal Y-E-S!"

More to the point, perhaps, <u>Thinner</u> is the first of the Bachman novels to move explicitly into Stephen King's territory: horror fantasy. It is also the first to appear in hardcover, as if it were intended to link the novels published under "Bachman" and those published under "King." The format of <u>Thinner</u> strongly suggests that King was preparing to "break" the news of the Bachman pseudonym; a novel so closely approximating his style, receiving the publicity and requiring the investment that <u>Thinner</u> did, seems a logical step toward acknowledging the pseudonym--a step Stephanie Leonard indicates King was preparing to take by March 1, 1985 (<u>Castle Rock</u> #3).

If that was King's intention, <u>Thinner</u> was the perfect vehicle. Readers have responded to the opening paragraph by asserting that only King could have created as effective a tone of horror. The gypsy's rotting, cancerous nose; the cloying sweetness of breath; lips like a wound and teeth like tombstones; the tongue slithering like something dark and evil--all evoke the particularly visceral horror of Stephen King. If the opening pages of <u>The Running Man</u> define that novel as science fiction, the opening paragraph of Thinner defines this one as horror.

As in Cujo, however, with its opening references to Frank Dodd and the monster in Tad Trenton's closet, Thinner begins by asserting horror, then calming the reader by a quick return to the commonplace: bacon and eggs frying for breakfast; Billy Halleck's quick glance at the scales and his momentary relief that his weight is down; brief family greetings at the breakfast table, masking a "shaky cease fire" between a husband and wife bickering over each other's problems with weight and cigarettes. The novel moves through increasingly complex narrative folds, revealing why the old gypsy of paragraph one touched Halleck's cheek and whispered a single word, "Thinner." Even so, King carefully controls the pacing, not allowing the novel to touch the conventions of horror until well into the middle chapters. Until then, he seems determined to keep the reader within the parameters of "normal" life.

This is, of course, a common technique in King's fiction. Horror fiction may approach its subject from two directions. The first is to work as Lovecraft, Poe, and others have done; the language of the opening lines establishes the horror. A story such as Lovecraft's "The Picture in the House" has virtually no plot: a traveler enters an old house and meets a strange man. There is a violent clap of thunder, and the house and the gentleman disappears. End of story.

The point lies not so much in narrative as in atmosphere. Words and phrases such as "searchers after horror," "catacombs," "mausolea," "nightmare countries," "black cobwebbed steps," "haunted wood and desolate mountain," and "sinister monoliths" prepare the reader for the assertion of horror in the final sentence of Lovecraft's first paragraph:

> But the true epicure in the terrible, to whom a new thrill of unutterable ghastliness is the chief end and justification of existence, esteems most of all the ancient, lonely farmhouses of backwoods New England; for there the dark

elements of strength, solitude, grotesqueness and ignorance combine to form the perfection of the hideous. (257)

In one paragraph, Lovecraft establishes that the narrative does not occur within what we consider "objective" reality; the evocative vocabulary and complex sentence structures create their own "reality."

An alternative technique, the one King frequently adopts, works in the opposite direction. The narrative may hint at horror, as do Thinner and Cujo, but concentrates on objectivity rather than subjectivity, on the everyday rather than on the weird and the "eldritch." King's publications preceding Thinner follow this pattern. Cujo begins by evoking Frank Dodd and the monster; almost immediately, however, it shifts to the Trenton's daily routine, to a realism of presentation that relieves the reader of the pressures imposed by the atmospheric imagery of a Lovecraft story. The Trentons belong to our world; we can imagine them because by and large they are us.

"Do the Dead Sing?," published in the same year as Cujo, gracefully combines the realistic with the supernatural in its compelling tale of an old woman encountering death. King could have (and has) treated the subject with less humanity and a greater sense of horror; not to do so, however, endows this story with a gentleness and a power that sets it above most tales of supernatural horror. It touches the reader on a new level, incorporating an intrusion of dark fantasy into the reality we know and understand. By starting at that level, King makes the fantastic not only acceptable but inevitable in the story.

Different Seasons carries the technique a step further. With one exception, the stories avoid supernatural horror. The most impelling of the four, "Apt Pupil" and "The Body," depend on the objective and the everyday to create an enduring sense of horror that transcends slimy ectoplasmic monsters.

Christine opens with a statement that defuses any sense of horror. The novel is about a "lover's triangle" composed of Arnie Cunningham (connections with the fifties and Happy Days were intentional), Leigh Cabot, and Christine. Readers first approaching the novel without having heard anything about it would have no reason to anticipate anything except a story of romantic entanglements. Only later, near the end of chapter one, does King reveal who (or what) Christine is. Even then, there is nothing implicitly horrific in the discovery that Christine is an automobile; after all, it is a truism that Americans have love affairs with their cars. King just takes the cliche and makes it literal to create a sense of horror that grows on the reader with the same speed and subtlety that it entraps Dennis and the others.

Even Pet Sematary, which received unusual publicity hype as being the novel that horrified even Stephen King, reflects the pattern. The novel was difficult for King to work with, as Winter indicates in The Art of Darkness. Yet even this novel, which represents in some sense an extreme of horror for writer and reader, skirts the horrific for nearly half its length. Even after Church has returned from the Pet Sematary substantially and eerily altered, the novel still invokes the real as much as the supernatural. Only in the last chapters, as the pace quickens and horror piles on horror, does the novel discard its realism of presentation and embrace the supernatural.

In this sense, Thinner is an archetypal King novel, opening with one perspective, concluding with quite another.

In addition, the novel includes secondary techniques that enhance the sense of psychological and physical realism. Several have been noted by earlier critics and reviewers; all appear in Thinner, not as tantalizing hints as to authorship but as fully developed narrative techniques essential to plot, character, and setting.

First, the novel is set in Maine. As in The Long Walk and The Running Man, the central character moves physically through a landscape familiar to King from his own life and to his readers through his novels. Bangor, Portland, Bar Harbor--all appear as Billy Halleck joins Ray Garraty and Ben Richards in fulfilling an odyssey of self-identity and survival.

Next, the novel exploits the potentials of italicized passages as counterpoint; typography becomes part of the narrative. This technique has drawn heavy fire from mainstream critics. Jack Sullivan's discussion of The Shining argues that King's problem is not simply that he is an inelegant writer; more fundamental is the fact that he becomes self-defeating, pretentious, in his use of typographic symbols:

> Sometimes non-punctuation or italics are used--quite arbitrarily--for gimmicky stream of consciousness effect. Occasionally we are subjected to all capitals in parentheses with triple exclamation points (!!!ON BOTH MARGINS!!!)! This is Mr. King's way of being climactic. (Qtd. in Gareffa, "Stephen King" 334)

The italics appear on the first page of Thinner, but to good purpose. They signal Billy Halleck's altering psychological states, memory differentiated from experience, rationality from the irrationality that tries to convince him that he is the object of a gypsy curse, while simultaneously writing Stephen King's signature with a flourish on each page.

In addition there is King's use of brand names, apparently a favorite with him since he refers frequently to himself as a "brand name" in horror. Billy Halleck does not simply eat junk food: he stuffs himself with Ritz crackers and Cheez-Doodles and Sara Lee cheesecakes and Whoppers and Ring Dings. His wife, Heidi, smokes Vantage 100's. King can label or name everything in Halleck's world; by doing so, he builds upon the world the reader experiences daily in the supermarket or while driving the gauntlet of urban billboards. Then, when the horror unfolds, it becomes a uniquely accessible horror; we have already accepted the world of the narrative as our own, with its brand names and concrete imagery. Once we have accepted that much, we are virtually forced to accept all of it, including the validity of gypsy curses. Much of *Thinner*, in fact, focuses on the potentials for horror we all face daily; the gypsy curse becomes critical only later in the novel.

At the same time, King does not separate the reader too insistently from the worlds of horror. Within the "realism" of brand names and everyday activities, he foreshadows disaster. Halleck and his wife make love, King tells us, adding the kicker: "For one of the last times" (58). The adumbrations do not reveal convolutions of plot. They merely remind us that all is not as it appears on the surface; beneath the "brand name" mentality of the characters and the worlds they inhabit lie other possibilities; in *The Talisman*, for example, such foreshadowings point to the parallel universe of the Territories, assuring the reader that what is to come is not a last minute aberration by the writer but part of a unified narrative. In *Thinner*, Ginelli does not appear until Chapter 21, two-thirds of the way through the narrative. By that time, Halleck is incapable of continuing action and the plot devolves onto Ginelli, with Halleck more spectator than actor; that situation has been suggested from the first chapter, however, when Halleck remembers that his first impulse after the accident was to call Ginelli. Even the strawberry pie of the final chapter is implicit in the novel, as King refers as early as page 116 to pies and plates and eating. In light of the novel's conclusion, the references are not only foreshadowings but disingenuous puns.

A final, occasionally superficial technique in King's fiction is his use of obscene or scatological language. This language may attract some readers; it certainly offends others. But King uses such language with care and discrimination. It is difficult to cite passages where the language is gratuitous. More frequently, harsh or crude language occurs when King needs them to create a characterization; in similar circumstances, other characters manage to communicate their meanings without recourse to non-standard usages. In *Thinner*, sexual references are more frequent and more explicit, however, since it depends upon sexuality for plot development: Billy Halleck´s guilt is extenuated by Heidi´s illicit actions in the car. The curse, as well as Billy´s attempted resolution of it, is a direct result of a sexual act.

In addition, bodily functions provide imagery throughout. When Ginelli tells about firing on the gypsy camp with a semi-automatic rifle and notes that any sleepers probably "made lemonade" in their sheets, the phrasing and the imagery immediately recall similar passages in *The Stand* and elsewhere. That image for urination has become another (if admittedly minor) signature piece for Stephen King.

All of these characteristics blend to give *Thinner* the unmistakable sense of a Stephen King novel. Even the content continues a series of investigations one might trace in King´s novels. *Carrie* was about a "haunted" girl; while her actions were extreme, psychokinesis itself remains a possibility. *´Salem´s Lot*, on the other hand, virtually locks the reader into the supernatural mode with its resurrection of the venerable vampire motif, while *The Shining* makes us believe again in haunted houses. *The Stand* moves back into the possible as it explores the consequences of our tampering with technology. *The Dead Zone* is about a haunted man, but Johnny Smith differs from us in only one way--he can perceive the future. *Firestarter* has another haunted child, one who can think flames into existence. *Cujo* is the most "realistic" of all; Cujo may be haunted by the revenant shade of Frank Dodd, but he has also been infected with rabies. With *Christine*, King touches a cherished American institution, the automobile, with the brush of horror. *Pet Sematary* depends upon our fear of death and our desire to circumvent it.

Thinner likewise gives us a haunting, and likewise connects it with elements of contemporary

125

life. In effect, King adds to his list of haunted people, haunted towns, haunted hotels, haunted dogs, and haunted cemeteries one more haunting--a haunted dieter.

Stated this bluntly, the idea seems absurd, as Mark Graham suggested when he referred to the plot as "off-the-wall," a phrase borrowed from the text itself. Yet <u>Thinner</u> manages to pull it off, because King does not simply begin with the curse and the haunting.

In its opening chapters, <u>Thinner</u> is more about contemporary fears, "real" fears, than about curses and vengeance. At first, Halleck is not particularly concerned about his weight loss; in fact, he is relieved. Like many Americans, he suffers from obesity; like many Americans, he understands the dangers of it but seems unable to do anything about it. His doctor, Michael Houston, says he is a heart attack waiting to happen, but all Billy can do is worry. He is incapable of acting. One measure designed to help insure his health has already backfired; he has quit smoking but by doing so has increased his weight even more.

Later, as he realizes that the weight is coming off too quickly in spite of his voracious eating, he re-focuses his fear. Obesity is only one problem. Cancer is another. First Halleck, then his wife, finally his doctor name their fear: cancer, the Big C. At this stage in the narrative, the disease functions literally; it represents one of the deepest fears we face. King allows that terror to surface in Billy Halleck. Only later, when Halleck has faced the truth about his problem, do the references to cancer become increasingly symbolic. For Halleck, there is something worse.

Once cancer has been eliminated as a possible cause, Halleck confronts a number of other potentially deadly diseases, contemporary forms of horror. Alzheimer's disease is mentioned, as is herpes. Halleck concentrates on <u>anorexia nervosa</u>, however, as the next most probable cause, evoking the spectre of Karen Carpenter as he wastes away (and simultaneously providing a clue as to when

Thinner was written). Finally, he must contend with cardiac arrythmia as his wasted body begins to malfunction.

In each case, King shows Halleck working through the sudden fear these diseases or conditions create and then reveals that whatever afflicts Halleck is even worse. Finally, when Halleck accepts the supernatural explanation, his wife, his doctor, and his co-workers must bear the terror of that final bug-bear of the modern world, mental illness. Since all other diagnoses have failed, Billy Halleck must be insane.

In this novel, horror may be as implicit in the familiar as in the exotic. In the beginning, the threat of cancer is just as unimaginable as the threat of a gypsy curse, and just as horrific. By Chapter 9, Halleck reacts to his bathroom scales as he would to any imaginary creature of horror: heart throbbing, head aching, eyes throbbing, teeth biting through his lip until the blood runs: "The image of the scale had taken on childish overtones of terror in his mind--the scale had become the goblin of his life" (69).

In Chapter 18, Halleck has reached Old Orchard Beach in his search for the gypsy caravan. As Halleck walks along the boardwalk, King describes the scene, consciously associating everyday objects with horror. A poodle is "grotesquely" fat. A "huge gull with mottled gray wings and dead black eyes" snatches a "greasy doughboy" from a child. Surrounding all is the "bone-white crescent" of the beach (165).

By the final chapters, Halleck has himself become an object of terror. Emaciated to near death, he shuffles toward a park bench for the final confrontation with the old gypsy, Taduz Lemke. In order to replenish his body's potassium, he has been eating oranges; he carries the bag with him, not noticing a small boy who runs from him while he is still half a block away. That night, King says, the boy would waken from a nightmare of a "shambling scarecrow with lifeless blowing hair on its skull-head [bearing] down on him." His mother, running to the sound of his cries, would hear him scream, "<u>It wants to make me</u>

eat oranges until I die! Eat oranges till I die! Eat till I die!" The progression is complete; Billy Halleck becomes the focus of horror. In an ironic inversion of theme, Halleck both embodies the gypsy's curse and passes it on.

Horror, says <u>Thinner</u>, comes in a variety of packages.

As in the earlier Bachman novels, King here develops a number of themes. For the first time, however, the themes represent fairly abstract issues. There is little of <u>The Running Man</u>'s diatribe against pollution, for example, or the indictment of the family at the core of <u>Rage</u>. Instead, <u>Thinner</u> seems more concerned with the interaction of two large generalizations: guilt and justice.

Characters are obsessed with assigning guilt. Taduz Lemke's daughter has been struck and killed by Billy Halleck's car. Someone must pay. Lemke identifies the guilty parties: Halleck, who was driving the car; Judge Cary Rossington, Halleck's friend, who controlled the courtroom and made certain that the incident would not stain Halleck's record or his own; and the Police Chief, Duncan Hopley, who failed to investigate the killing thoroughly. In the eyes of the ancient Lemke, these three must suffer retribution. He touches each and speaks a single word, calling down curses as punishment and vengeance. For him, the question is simple, the resolution direct.

Halleck, however, faces a deep ambivalence. Once he accepts Lemke's curse as the cause of his rapid and continuous weight loss, he must confront his own guilt and that of others. When he speaks to Hopley (in near darkness, because of the particular effects the curse has on Hopley's complexion), Halleck accepts his own portion of blame. He was driving, he admits, and his car struck and killed the old woman. There was no drinking or drugs involved, he assures Hopley; instead, his "wife of sixteen years picked that day to give [him] a handjob in the car" (115) . . . the first and only time. Guilt, he realizes, is fluid. Rossington and his wife blame

Halleck for Rossington's affliction, something out of fifties' films like The Hideous Sun Demon; Hopley blames Halleck. Lemke and his grandchildren blame Halleck, Rossington, and Hopley. But Halleck insists that guilt be shared by all. Heidi must accept a portion; without her action, he would have been able to stop in time. Rossington and Hopley are guilty in that they did not prosecute or investigate the death diligently. Eventually, he argues that Lemke and his daughter are also to blame, he for bringing the caravan to Fairview, she for stepping out between the cars. Maybe, he concludes, "we should all just lay it off on fate or destiny" (115) rather than struggling to assign guilt. In human affairs, the novel seems to say, guilt is rarely simple.

Nor is justice. If the question of guilt causes Lemke's curse, the desire for justice underlies it. The novel, however, shows that justice is itself slippery and difficult to control.

The issue first arises indirectly and ironically, in a manner appropriate to what Gray calls King's "postliterate" style. Halleck and his wife have returned from a brief honeymoon-like vacation. His weight loss has become noticeable, and he has begun to worry about it. In one of their last nights of domestic peace, they eat Sara Lee cheesecake and watch And Justice for All on television. That title becomes a leitmotif throughout Thinner as characters attempt to apportion justice in an unjust, uncaring, and at times deviously ironic universe. Halleck's odyssey through Maine becomes a search for justice of a narrow sort, designed to lighten his own burden and spread it out over others. King treats the question literally as he describes Rossington's curse in a chapter aptly and ironically called "The Scales of Justice." Rossington is a judge, in this instance a judge who has made himself blind to certain elements of the case. What better punishment than that he develop literal scales.

Lemke and the gypsies have a more active conception of justice. They do not receive it from others; instead, they must make their own. When Halleck meets with Lemke for the first time, Lemke greets him contemptuously. The man has killed his daughter. The law has done nothing. But the gypsy knows who did what and has taken appropriate steps. Hopley and Rossington are dead; Halleck will soon follow. Halleck demands to know whether that sort of justice will bring Lemke's dead daughter back to life. Lemke replies that he does not need the dead to return; he needs justice, something quite different.

Halleck shifts from arguing guilt and justice to arguing that the balance is now even, what they call a "push" in Las Vegas. He killed Susanna Lemke; she crossed between two cars. She is dead; his life has been altered radically and permanently. Questions of justice and guilt become moot. It is a push.

At this point, the novel takes a startling turn. Thus far, Halleck has worked through the possibilities he knows and understands, the diseases that could result in his life-threatening weight loss, only to discover that the only logical alternative remaining him is the most illogical and irrational one: he is under a curse. The curse results from his guilt and represents a rough attempt at justice.

When Lemke refuses to accept Halleck's reasoning and threatens to strengthen the curse, Halleck accepts the challenge. Make it worse, he demands. Lemke falters, and Halleck responds with his own curse, the "curse of the white men from town" (199). To his surprise, Lemke reacts with fear. The scales of justice have reversed; the question of guilt has rebounded to Lemke. In denying what Halleck asked for, he steps beyond the boundaries of justice into vengeance, giving Halleck the chance to discover that he too has the power to curse.

Halleck's curse is Richard Ginelli, a mafioso type reminiscent of Cressner in "The Ledge," Correzente in "The Man With a Belly," Mike Scollay in "The Wedding Gig," Dolan in "Dolan's Cadillac," or Salvatore Magliore in <u>Roadwork</u>. Although King has alluded to Ginelli since the opening chapters of the novel, the character now appears for the first time, supplanting Halleck as focal character until the final three chapters. He is the mover and the actor, the agent by which Lemke's curse is neutralized . . . or at least shifted, since a curse is like a living thing. It cannot simply be removed; it must be given to someone else.

Ginelli is indeed the "curse of the white men from town." He becomes as immovable and dispassionate as Lemke's original curse. If Lemke's curse first effected Halleck by reminding him of the terrors implicit within modern society in the form of multiple diseases, Ginelli reminds the gypsies of their insecurity, of the threats they have faced for generations from the people of the towns. The first night, he destroys valuable property as a warning; the second night he fires on their camp, careful not to harm anyone, but equally careful to roust them all and let them know that danger threatens. The third night, he threatens Lemke's own family. Lemke recognizes the inplacability of Halleck's curse and capitulates. He promises to show Halleck how to remove the curse.

At this point, the novel seems to have concluded. Guilt has been exonerated through suffering and the balance of justice restored. Halleck even knows who should now receive a full measure of the pulsing curse . . . and how.

But there are still three chapters remaining. In those chapters, King shows how very wrong Halleck is. Justice does not triumph, not in a universe in which gypsy curses become embedded in strawberry pies. Halleck may have been able to call down his own curse, but he cannot control Lemke's once it passes into his possession. The final chapter, the final page reminds us of the world of <u>Pet Sematary</u>, with a closing statement almost as paralyzing as King's

> A cold hand fell on Louis' shoulder. Rachel's voice was grating, full of dirt.
> "<u>Darling</u>," it said. (373)

Thinner concludes with an act as domestic as a wife laying her hand on her husband's shoulder and calling him "darling" . . . and as chillingly horrific.

Guilt and justice become largely irrelevant in Halleck's world.

A secondary theme in *Thinner* deals with the outsider. It is appropriate, in light of King's discussion of the outsider in *Danse Macabre* that many of King's characters are outsiders, especially in the Bachman novels: Charlie Decker, Ray Garraty, Ben Richards. Others become outsiders: Barton George Dawes . . . and William Halleck.

The theme appears early in the novel as Halleck and his family picnic on the common and watch the police harrass gypsies. Linda later asks why the police wouldn't let them stay. Halleck answers with evasions and half-truths; Ginelli, Halleck knows, would tell Linda the truth, that "you got to keep the undesirables out of town, sweetness" (48). And the gypsies are undesirables.

Halleck accepts that classification, since he is one of the desirables. He belongs. He has a fine home on an exclusive street in an exclusive neighborhood. He has a beautiful wife, a lovely daughter, a big, powerful car. He wears the right clothes. When he meets Michael Houston at the local bar, the Watering Hole, Houston wears red golfing pants and white shoes, the local costume. King has used that combination before as a way of signaling those who belong; in *Cujo* for example, the "head Honcho" from the Maine Realtors' Association wears red pants and white shoes; Donna Trenton wears white shorts and a red-checked blouse after she rejects Steve Kemp as her lover and returns to being the model Maine housewife. Halleck recognizes the symbolic colors and what they stand for as he looks down and sees his own white shoes. "Who are you kidding," he asks himself. "You wear the tribal feather" (40).

Overweight, suburbanite lawyers are in; ancient gypsies and their caravans of campers and vans are not.

Halleck discovers, however, how transient

such categories can be. He loses weight. At
first this accentuates his sense of belonging.
After all, being fit is also a preoccupation of
suburban America. As the weight loss continues,
though, he becomes more and more the outsider.
When his co-workers think he has cancer, he
becomes invisible; they grant his request for a
leave of absense with relief, eager to have him
out of sight. As he becomes thinner, his daughter
cannot stand to see him; she leaves home to stay
with a friend. Finally, when he becomes convinced
that he is cursed, his remaining friends (with one
exception) desert him, his wife and doctor have
him declared insane, and passersby treat him as a
circus sideshow freak. Halleck has become an
outsider.

His only connection with his previous life is
Ginelli, who is also an outsider. A marginally
respectable mobster, Ginelli has remained friends
with Halleck at a distance, so that his own
disreputable dealings might not injure Halleck´s
standing as a lawyer. When Halleck calls for
help, however, Ginelli comes, eventually sacri-
ficing his life for Halleck´s. The outsider
suddenly understands what it is to be isolated
. . . and to have a friend.

As Halleck´s odyssey continues, he discovers
how critical the outsider is. "We need the gypsies," says an internal voice as Halleck waits for
Taduz Lemke to arrive. "Because if you don´t have
someone to run out of town once in a while, how
are you going to know you yourself belong
there" (276).

The theme climaxes when Halleck returns home.
He has gained some weight; more importantly, he
has the curse safely contained in a still-warm,
pulsating strawberry pie. Heidi meets him on
their front step; she wears a red skirt and
sleeveless white blouse, the appropriate uniform
for those who belong. He looks at her and understands the depth of change in himself. He is now
more gypsy than white man from town, he realizes.
The experiences have altered him in more ways than
physically. He is an outsider, and nothing can
bring him back again. His one hope, his daughter

Linda, proves as illusory as any other.

Given Halleck's state at the end of the novel, the conclusion is terrifying . . . and, ironically, inevitable. He cannot return to what he was.

A number of other themes develop in Thinner. The novel focuses intensely on cancer as contemporary object of horror, as was the case in the earlier Bachman novels. Here, however, it is more personal and direct. In Roadwork, Dawes' son died of cancer; in The Running Man, Richards meets a boy whose five-year-old sister is dying of cancer. In Thinner, Halleck himself confronts the threat and survives the accompanying panic. What has before functioned imagistically and symbolically becomes an actual threat the protagonist must face. Only when King works through that fear does Halleck confront the next level of terror: the supernatural.

Thinner also deals with sexuality, particularly sexuality as threat. As in narratives such as The Long Walk and "The Raft," intercourse leads to death. Heidi's illicit actions in the car cause Susanna Lemke's death; indirectly all of the other characters are touched by and eventually destroyed by the subsequent interlocking curses. From the beginning, Halleck identifies an overt expression of sexuality with his own problem, transferring a portion of his guilt to Heidi. Even as Halleck makes love to Heidi, he hates her.

That hatred, coupled with King's attitudes toward sexuality, condemns Halleck's family to the same disintegration we have seen in the other Bachman novels. There are, of course, variations here. Billy Halleck wants to protect his daughter. From the beginning, he tries to protect her from harsh realities, from a world where fathers can run down old gypsy women in the streets. Again and again, he lies to her to soften fact, not quite realizing how much she has grown and how much she understands. When he leaves home to track the gypsies down, he unknowingly recapitulates the actions of absent fathers throughout King's fictions. He has not willingly abandoned Linda, but he has no alternatives. To remain at home is tantamount to death, as it is for Ben Richards in The Running Man. So he leaves, breaking irrevocably an already fragile family relationship. In his absence, Heidi has him declared insane and tries to have him committed; Linda fights with her mother and leaves home; and Halleck becomes convinced of his wife's culpability for all that has happpened and literally plots her murder.

Throughout the novel, he argues that Linda's innocence should protect her from any involvement in the curse. He shields her from too much knowledge of what is happening. But not even those best intentions succeed. By the end of the novel, the family is together again, but ironically and horribly.

Thinner also uses a number of techniques familiar to King's readers. The novel is allusive, but not as insistently as The Long Walk or Roadwork. Halleck is an educated man; his narrative includes casual references to authors as disparate as Louis L'Amour; John D. MacDonald, an appropriate choice in light of the detective-thriller context of the novel at that point; Judy Blume; Maurice Sendak; Dorothy Sayers; Herman Melville; and, obliquely, Ernest Hemingway. What is missing, however, is a central literary figure to help shape and structure the novel, as Shirley Jackson or Ernest Hemingway had done in The Long Walk or Roadwork.

If Thinner does owe that kind of literary debt to a single writer, it would have to be to King himself. In Thinner, King paraphrases his own novels and stories, most frequently The Talisman. The large narrative movements of the two novels share several similarities. Characters in trouble (both difficulties stemming from ill health, possibly cancer) seek help by moving through parallel worlds. In The Talisman, Jack Sawyer's Territories represent an alternate, high-fantasy world. In Thinner Billy Halleck remains in this physical universe, but becomes part of a psychological parallel reality in which gypsy curses work. Both Jack Sawyer and Billy Halleck return to their original frame bearing an object infused with power from the parallel world: Sawyer's glowing globe, and Halleck's strawberry pie. Both confront and defeat powerful enemies with the help of friends who are themselves dangerous. Both are ultimately helpless, the first because of his age, the second because of his physical debilitation. They must depend upon others, although the final actions must be their own. The sense of the quest, of a rite of passage leading to self-identification, is strong in both novels.

There are, in addition, a number of lesser similarities, recurrent images and motifs that both novels share. Cancer, of course, is critical to both, but even objects as superficial as sneakers, emblems of unicorns, Oshkosh jeans, Ring Dings and Burger King Whoppers, coke-sniffing villains, and characters suffering from virulent cases of acne connect the two novels. Halleck's dream-vision of Fairview and the vulture, with the people he knows (including a brief appearance by Ronald Reagan) dying of starvation parallels the description of Point Venuti in _The Talisman_. Even the occurrence of strawberries becomes important. In _The Talisman_, one of the first people in the Territories to threaten Jack Sawyer is the palace chef. He screams in a thin, flutey voice, with an accent reminiscent of Lemke's: "Ged-OUT!" One of the kitchen women upsets a pie-rack and a strawberry pie falls out: "Strawberry juice splattered and ran, the red as fresh and bright as arterial blood" (94-95). In _Thinner_, Lemke's pie contains a "swimming viscous fluid in which dark things--strawberries, maybe--floated like clots" (278). In each instance, strawberry pies are associated with blood, with threat, with an intrusion of the fantastic.

There are, of course, major differences as well. _The Talisman_ is an epic quest-fantasy and meets the formal requirements of that genre, disappointing many readers who might have expected supernatural horror. _Thinner_, on the other hand, is a horror novel. After the opening paragraph, King retreats temporarily into scenes of contemporary life. But gradually he begins re-creating the horror that readers expect of him as Halleck sets out on his quest for the gypsy caravan. If anything disappoints in _Thinner_, it could only be that those who had read and enjoyed the earlier "Bachman" novels might miss the psychological suspense that King experimented with so successfully there.

   This, then, is _Thinner_, the last of King's "Richard Bachman" novels. With this novel, he integrates the Bachman canon with the novels published under his own name. _Thinner_ carries to a conclusion many of the themes, images, and techniques King had explored in the non-horror context of _Rage_, _The Long Walk_, _Roadwork_, and _The Running Man_, but in _Thinner_ King returns to horror fantasy. Having demonstrated his ability to write mainstream fiction, not only in stories such as "Apt Pupil," "The Body," "Rita Hayworth and Shawshank Redemption," "The Last Rung," and "The Woman in the Room," but also in the Bachman novels, King has achieved a great deal. To paraphrase Paul Gray's concluding remarks about _Different Seasons_, the Bachman novels may not win King critical respect, but they do show that there is more to him than just a master of horror fantasy. Each of the novels, including _Thinner_, allows King to develop greater depth, from the rather flat characterizations in _Rage_ to more rounded personalities in _Thinner_; from straight-line narrative in _Rage_ and _The Long Walk_ to convoluted narratives in _The Running Man_ and _Thinner_; from rather adolescent attempts at philosophizing in _Rage_ to more complex views of reality in _Roadwork_ and _Thinner_.

   The addition of these five novels to King's canon provides more evidence of King's versatility. It is both appropriate and exciting that he has acknowledged them.

Chapter VIII

SPECULATIONS

King has now acknowledged publishing as "John Swithen" and "Richard Bachman." His identifying himself as the author of the Bachman novels had two immediate results: sales of Thinner spiraled . . . and old rumors resurfaced.

After all, many readers have wondered, if he admits to two pen names, could there not be more? Castle Rock has assured readers that there are no more pen names: "As to whether or not he has any other pseudonyms," Stephanie Leonard writes, "except for using the name John Swithen . . . for one short story, he has never used any other pseudonym. Really . . . Trust me . . ." (#4, 1). Yet when King was asked on Good Morning America if there were others waiting to be discovered, he replied rather hesitantly, "No comment . . . I don´t think so" (12 April 1985). His reticence may give new life to several long-standing suppositions:

* Stephen King wrote an occult novel, Exorcism, under the pen-name "Eth Natas." The novel was published in 1972 by Lexington, then republished by Manor in 1974.

* Stephen King wrote a science-fiction novel, Invasion, under the pen-name "Aaron Wolfe." This novel was published in 1975 by Laser, with a foreword admitting that "Wolfe" was a pseudonym.

* Stephen King wrote a science-fiction novel rejected by DAW. It was so bad that he even destroyed correspondence referring to it.

* Stephen King wrote two sets of five novels, one science fiction, one suspense thrillers.

Invasion may have been one of the science-fiction novels.

* Stephen King wrote at least two Westerns, a rumor given greater credence by "Slade" and The Dark Tower.

The situation has also invited new speculations. There is , for instance, a rumor that King is his own secretary. Stephanie Leonard commented in the March 1985 issue of Castle Rock that

> several people have intimated recently that my handwriting, especially my signature, is a lot like S.K.'s, one even saying that it was "masculine." I wonder if they were hinting at something, and finally one person told me he had decided that I was a pseudonym Stephen King used at times (Stephanie being the feminine form of Stephen, Leonard being derived from lion, the King of Beasts!). (#3, 1)

"Not true," she concludes, "Ask anyone who's talked to me on the phone."

Now, it seems, additional rumors are being invented, part of a widespread "pseudonym-craze." Purcell's conclusion that John Wilson's Love Lessons is an early King novel created both interest and consternation. The review explicitly links King's name to the series of erotic novels published while King was "selling short stories to men's magazines" (31). The fact that his stories and articles have appeared in Cavalier, Gent, Gallery, Playboy, and Penthouse, coupled with King's occasional references to the Penthouse "Forum" in stories and interviews, makes it seem at least possible that he might have written such novels. According to Robert Collins, editor of Fantasy Review, however, the entire review--book title, publisher, reviewer--was a hoax by Charles Platt and Neil Barron. Although Fantasy Review has published a disclaimer, the rumor that King wrote erotic novels will no doubt continue to surface, along with the others.

These rumors, and others like them, are so persistent in fact that it might be worthwhile to examine several, to see why certain books continue to be unofficially linked to King's name, in spite of his frequent denials.

As far as the two Westerns go, King has tried writing Westerns. "Slade," an early story available only on microfilm from the University of Maine at Orono, is a tongue-in-cheek Western that reveals both King's sense of humor and his engagement with the genre. The characters in The Dark Tower also frequently reflect King's interest in Westerns, even to his sub-title, "The Gunslinger." In spite of this, however, King says that he has never published a Western as such. In a recent note, he indicated that he tried a Western once, but "it died after 20,000 words. It was pretty good, too--I love the form." One of the characters in his forthcoming The Tommyknockers, he continues, is a writer of Western novels.

The manuscript submitted to DAW was in fact The Running Man, rejected not because of any intrisic literary failings but because DAW did not publish "negative utopias." Nor was the correspondence destroyed--it was merely lost over the years.

Discounting the highly amorphous stories of whole series of pseudonymous novels (difficult to accept both because of their vagueness and King's enormous output of published materials), there remain only two serious contenders: Exorcism and Invasion.

"Eth Natas" must surely rank among the most obviously fictitious names in publishing. A novel called Exorcism by "The Satan" meets the first criteria for investigation: it is certainly pseudonymous. Whether it is King's, however, is another matter.

A number of bookdealers specializing in fantasy have linked King to this novel. Late, late one evening, several years ago, King is supposed to have admitted to a small group that he wrote Exorcism. No one seems to know any more about the occasion, and King has denied the story, but the connection between King and this novel remains alive nonetheless.

Even a brief look at Exorcism, however, reveals few internal clues pointing to King. The book is, to quote one reader, "execrable"; more generously, it is highly stereotypic in language, characterization, and plot. More to the point, there is little to suggest King's hand in it. The setting is atypical: Manhattan, instead of King's usual Maine. King has occasionally used other settings than New England; The Shining, The Stand and stories such as "The Breathing Method" illustrate this. Bentley Morton's home, Whitestone, is appropriate to a horror novel, with its forbidding exterior in the Dracula style of architectural embellishment, but there is nothing specific to suggest King's imagination.

The style is also inappropriate; from the first words the novel seems old-fashioned, more leisurely than King's usual. True, he has explored alternative styles, as in "The Man Who Would Not Shake Hands," but again, there is little here to suggest King specifically. In addition, the novel uses a first-person narrator, unlike most of King's novels, including all the Bachman novels except Rage.

Even more significant, however, is the lack of distinctive characteristics. The sense of the concrete is missing, even from passages which would invite brand names. The first chapter begins with a quoted sign, as did The Long Walk and Roadwork; here there is no follow-up, however. It remains an isolated incident. The reference to a disastrous accident in the Peruvian Andes intrudes the unnecessarily exotic into the narrative, something foreign to King. His horrors may terrify, they may be outré and inexplicable, but they usually depend more upon horror within the commonplace than upon geographical distance. To mention the Peruvian Andes in most King narratives would be to introduce an element of the ludicrous.

Even this brief discussion of Exorcism suggests little evidence for King's authorship. If he did write it, he presumably did so before he developed the traits that characterize his writing.

The case is more complex with <u>Invasion</u>, however. Although King has denied authorship (Stephanie Leonard says it is "very safe" to say it is not by King), <u>Invasion</u> is occasionally mentioned as another King "possible." It is an unprepossessing novel, with little to differentiate it from other works by unknown authors, but for several years, it has sometimes been attributed to King.

Initially, the text is ambiguous. Readers react immediately to the opening pararaph of <u>Thinner</u>, with its visceral evocation of stench and decay. As one reader put it, how could it be by anyone except Stephen King. There is nothing as obvious in <u>Invasion</u>. The style is restrained, the sentences long and carefully structured, suggesting a rational, objective first-person narrator.

Yet there are a few intriguing details. <u>Invasion</u> recounts an alien attack on an isolated family, snowed in on a farmhouse in rural Maine, King's country. Even an image as commonplace as berries could connect <u>Invasion</u> to King. Toby Hanlon's pony is named Blueberry. Blueberries and strawberries occur frequently in King's fictions: "Strawberry Spring," "Children of the Corn," and "I Know What You Need" among the short stories; the strawberry juice "fresh as arterial blood" in <u>The Talisman</u> (95); <u>Thinner</u>'s sinister strawberry pie; the "splash of blueberry drool" that results from Carrie's telekinesis (7); the seductively homey "strawberry tart or blueberry buckle" in <u>Roadwork</u> (26); the single blueberry in the puzzle in <u>Rage</u> (117). The point is not, however, that they occur; after all, any one can mention strawberries or blueberries. In King, though, berries seem peculiarly ambivalent. On the surface, they suggest warm domesticity; underneath, they symbolize isolation and terror. "Strawberry Spring" describes violent death. The soda and pie in "I Know What You Need" and "Children of the Corn" hide deeper horrors. Halleck's pie transfers the gypsy curse. Carla Ordner's blueberry buckle helps

Steve Ordner manipulate truth and integrity. The blueberry puzzle, the last berry in the field, emphasizes Decker´s mother´s disengagement from normal affections. And Toby Hanlon´s pony Blueberry is an image both of pleasure and of horror: her yellow-stained bones trigger Hanlon´s irrational fear of the aliens.

<u>Invasion</u> also emphasizes eyes. For most of the novel, we do not see the aliens, only reflections from their eyes: huge, amber, saucer-shaped, glowing through the Maine darkness. In <u>Carrie</u>, Billy Nolan and his friends smoke joints that glow like "the lambent eyes of some rotating Cerberus" (89). Later, cigarettes wink like demons´ eyes (104). Margaret White´s grandmother´s eyes glowed with a "kind of witch´s light" when the Devil´s power was on her (120); outside the gymnasium, Billy Nolan´s eyes glow "ferally" (126). In "Mrs. Todd´s Shortcut," Mrs. Todd has "brown eyes just like lamps" (181) and a forehead that shone like a lamp (188); one of the creatures she kills had "big yellowy eyes" (187) like the aliens in <u>Invasion</u>. A similar emphasis on eyes occurs in "I Know What You Need," with its "red hurricane-lamp eyes" (233); in the "something green with terrible red eyes the size of footballs" in "Children of the Corn" (276); in "eyes huge and red, like spirit lamps" in "Big Wheels" (188); in eyes "like lanterns being waved aimlessly in the dark" in "The Raft" (38, 39); and in "lamplike green eyes" from <u>Cycle of the Werewolf</u>. In King, eyes are frequently large, saucer-shaped, flaring red or yellow like lamps, just as they are in <u>Invasion</u>.

The Hanlons fit the pattern for King´s typical families: father, mother, one child. In <u>Rage</u>, <u>The Long Walk</u>, <u>Roadwork</u>, <u>The Running Man</u>, and <u>Thinner</u>, as well as <u>Carrie</u>, <u>´Salem´s Lot</u>, <u>The Stand</u>, <u>The Shining</u>, <u>The Dead Zone</u>, <u>Firestarter</u>, <u>Cujo</u>, and <u>Christine</u>, we find limited families. Only rarely, as in <u>The Eyes of the Dragon</u>, <u>Cycle of the Werewolf</u>, "The Body," or "Gramma" does King work beyond the basic three members. Where there are brothers or sisters, they are generally threats, as in "The Body." The name, <u>Hanlon</u>, provides yet another possible connection: one of the characters in King's *It* is (coincidentally) named "Mike Hanlen."

Such points, of course, do not constitute proof of authorship. They only suggest parallels that might repay further consideration. More critical, however, are other elements, including style.

One stylistic device that immediately suggests King is his use of brand names; certainly such names in *Thinner* led many readers to suspect his hand in it. *Invasion* is more restrained, perhaps as one might expect. Since the novel is pseudonymous, one might expect some muting of style, whether King's or another writer's. Still, there are touches. Places are carefully named, the names used whenever possible: Timberlake Farm and Pastor's Hill, for example. Hanlon also says that he survived a difficult ordeal "with the aid of a fifth of Wild Turkey bourbon [and] a box of No-Doz caffeine tablets" (185).

A more significant stylistic index is the use of interruptives. King frequently interrupts characters' speech with parenthetical or italicized passages so that speech and narration parallel thought, literally and graphically on the page, as in this passage from *Carrie*:

> And suddenly it broke. The horrible realization of how badly she had been cheated came over her, and a horrible, soundless cry
> (they're LOOKING at me)
> tried to come out of her. (149)

Invasion uses this stylistic strategy only rarely in the first chapters, where Hanlon preserves the facade of rationality for as long as possible, explaining away odd happenings until there are no more explanations but one: aliens have invaded and are killing people. As his own sanity is tested, Hanlon interpolates passages for continuity and clarity. He does not interrupt sentences, as King did in *Carrie* and *The Shining*. Instead, the passages are long, fit between complete statements. But they create a fragmented, interrupted narrative; as in King's novels, ideas are separated by passages ringing variations on those ideas, giving the illusion of complexity.

In a related technique, *Invasion* transforms reality by using stychometric repetition and inversion. The best example in King's novels is Danny Torrance's

> REDRUM.
> MURDER.
> REDRUM.
> MURDER.

from *The Shining* (307). In *Invasion*, the same technique appears more expansively and with greater variation. Hanlon parallels his experiences in Vietnam with his experiences in the novel; his reactions to both require a litany against death:

> Death is not beatable.
> Death is not cheatable.
> Death is not mutable.
> Death is real and final. (128)

The actual sequence continues for almost two pages (104-105)

To this point, while there are suggestions of King in *Invasion*, there is nothing definitive. And, while *Invasion* is contemporary (in publication date at any rate) with King's *Carrie* and *'Salem's Lot*, it belongs to a different genre: science fiction. The shift from science fiction to horror fantasy alters perspectives, purposes, structures, narrative techniques, and vocabulary. Science fiction emphasizes technology and science--in a word, the external. Horror, on the other hand, depends upon the irrational, the subjective, and the internal. If *Invasion* were a pseudonymous work by Stephen King, the choice of genres could explain a number of anomalies in the novel.

When the aliens finally reveal themselves, breaking through windows into the house, they seem more creatures from a 1950s horror film than science fiction aliens. They blend mantis and grasshopper: seven-foot-tall insectoids with eight legs, a two-foot-wide head, and two saucer-sized yellow eyes (165-166), resembling creatures in such films as Them! (1954), The Deadly Mantis (1957), The Beginning of the End (1957) or Tarantula (1955), films King refers to in Danse Macabre and Night Shift as horror films disguised as science fiction. That genealogy also suggests King's "The Mist" (1980).

More to the point, the creatures recall what Charlie Decker sees in Rage: "The elongated shadow-heads on the tent wall bobbed up and down, back and forth, with insectile glee. They didn't look like people at all. They looked like a bunch of talking praying mantises . . . . Dark, fear, firelight, shadows like praying mantises" (13, 15). In The Long Walk, Garraty sees powerline supports where men hang "like grotesque praying mantises" (236). And in Roadwork, Dawes sees his nemesis, the wrecking crane, as a mantis caught up in some "unknown period of contemplation" (162), symbolizing its implicit, quiescent potential for horror. As King had done for the literary vampire in 'Salem's Lot, Invasion gives the 1950's creature new life. As in 'Salem's Lot, the creature is withheld until well into the book. In final effect as well, the aliens of Invasion relate more to the horror in 'Salem's Lot or The Shining than to Gort or Klaatu, the SF aliens in The Day the Earth Stood Still (1951).

The novel is classified as "science fiction," but the technologies involved are never explained. Animals are stripped of flesh without any bloodletting; the aliens refuse to explain how or why. Animals and humans are controlled by the aliens; yet nowhere does Wolfe explain how the aliens control animals or how (if alien and human are so mutually non-understandable) they form human thoughts. In a science fiction novel, such lapses could be devastating; indeed, many science-fiction novelists would concentrate on precisely those problems. In a horror novel, however, the lapses would be virtually demanded. Horror is effective when it asserts, not when it explains. It is one thing to discover a pony's skeleton in the snow, the bones stained as if dipped into acid, with no blood or flesh to be seen. Such an episode could, and does, create horror. To explain how and why aliens accomplished it would deflate the horror with an intellectual response. But *Invasion* is visceral, both in the narrative and in its effect on the reader. As such, it relates more to horror novels than to most science fiction.

Invasion does, however, suggest connections with *'Salem's Lot*, published the same year. Both novels are set in an isolated Maine landscape. The central characters are writers. Hanlon has written one book, a diary of his experiences in Vietnam. At the end of *Invasion*, he completes another novel, written under compulsion and designed to make the events of the novel understandable, if not to the aliens then to himself. "If we survive the ordeal at Timberlake Farm," he says, "I could best cleanse my soul of the stain if I put the story down on paper" (106). Mears is similarly impelled to write the third novel, even after his publisher rejects the outline.

In both *Invasion* and *'Salem's Lot*, the battle narrows to three parties: the man, the boy, and the alien. In each, the woman is lost, as are friends and neighbors. King's Jimmy Cody dies from multiple wounds as he falls into the cellar of Mrs. Miller's boarding house, and, although King does not describe his death, the means and resulting image resemble Connie Hanlon's death:

> The thing was on her in an instant, clutching her with its forelegs, plunging the stinger into her stomach. The razored tip of it came out of her back, streaming blood and yellow ichor. (176)

King uses kitchen knives embedded in plywood, but the result is the same.

Such similarities, however, cannot disguise differences between the two. *Invasion* is more streamlined, involving only three people. Their one outside contact, a telephone call, ends abruptly. 'Salem's Lot encompasses an entire town. In addition, 'Salem's Lot is less optimistic. Ben Mears and Mark Petrie escape but are scarred emotionally and psychologically. Invasion is more optimistic, but also ambivalent. Connie Hanlon is not dead . . . or rather, she was dead and is resurrected by the aliens' nameless technology. Humanity wins in spite of its flaws and weaknesses. In an inversion of everything Hanlon had discovered in Vietnam, he now knows that death is not final, that the universe is a madhouse: "As Toby and I sat on the edge of the bed and the three of us hugged one another, the night was filled with our maniacal but undeniably happy laughter" (190).

The connections between Invasion and The Shining, published two years later, are more precise. In some ways, Invasion could stand as an early draft for the later novel, moving toward science fiction rather than horror.

King's article, "On The Shining and Other Perpetrations," says that The Shining evolved over ten years, including his early intention to write a novel reflecting Bradbury's, "The Veldt"; later, in 1972, he thought of a novel called Darkshine, set in an amusement park. Two years later, while in Colorado, he dreamed of his son being chased down a hotel corridor by a fire-hose: "I got up, lit a cigarette, sat in the chair looking out the window at the Rockies, and by the time the cigarette was done, I had the bones of the book firmly set in my mind" (13).

Sometime during that gestation, other treatments might have suggested themselves. Given parallels in plot, characterization, setting, theme, motif, symbol, and style between Invasion and The Shining, such seems at least possible. In each, three people (father, mother, son) are isolated by winter storms. They cannot contact others directly until after the crisis has passed. The fathers are debilitated. Hanlon has suffered from war-induced catatonia. Connie and Toby speak carefully, avoiding references to Vietnam or to his hospitalization. King's Jack Torrance is equally handicapped psychologically, equally subect to Wendy's censure and frequent distrust; like Hanlon, he has to prove himself. His problems are alcoholism and the urge to child-abuse. King emphasizes Jack's psychological scars when he writes that

> By making Jack Torrance a drinker who was trying to quit and by making him a part of the insidous [sic] child-beating syndrome that is passed from father to son to grandson, I found myself able to look around a dark corner and to see myself as I could have been, under the right set of circumstances. ("On The Shining" 14)

Because Jack's terrors are internal, writing <u>The Shining</u> became a "ritual burning," a purgation that King says "flowed, almost whole, from [his] subconscious" (14), hypnotic and extraordinary. Perhaps because <u>Invasion</u> was published under a pen-name, it lacks that sense.

The fathers also differ, however. Hanlon misudges his relationship with his wife and son, the effects of isolation on the family, and the nature of the enemy he must defeat. He loses; the aliens kill Connie and abduct Toby. In a larger sense, however, he wins. He regains both Toby and Connie. Jack Torrance also misjudges everything around him; his errors, however, lead to death. The horrors within overcome him, until he joins the evil and attempts to kill his wife and son. The Overlook wins Jack; Wendy and Danny barely escape.

The boys are named Toby and Danny. Hanlon's first name is Don; Danny Torrance's imaginary friend is Tony--names only a letter different ("Hanlon," "Hatlen," and "Hallorann" are not much further apart). Both boys act older than they are, a common trait in King's fiction. In <u>The Shining</u>, <u>Pet Sematary</u>, <u>The Eyes of the Dragon</u>, or <u>The Talisman</u>, for example, King's children are like the children in Renaissance court paintings, miniature adults in adult garb.

The plots of <u>Invasion</u> and <u>The Shining</u> require

this greater maturity, since the sons are the crux in each. Toby Hanlon is a child, his mind easy to control. The final chapter refers to the "Toby-alien," showing how completely the two identities have coalesced. Through Toby, speaking for the aliens, Hanlon comes to understand himself. Danny Torrance is likewise critical. In spite of Jack's misunderstandings about his own importance, the Overlook really wants Danny. In both novels, the action revolves around keeping the son safe. Again, of course, there is the fundamental difference: in one, the father works for the son's welfare; in the other, against it.

Settings are also similar: open spaces, snow-covered distances, isolation. The farmhouse Hanlon rents is more than a farmhouse, just as the Overlook is more than a hotel. Timberlake Farm is a miniature Overlook, larger than necessary, more pretentious than its location would demand. Even the names, like Don and Danny or Toby and Tony, echo: <u>Timberlake</u> and <u>Overlook</u>.

Death itself provides an additional connection. Connie Hanlon's death is graphic in a novel in which skeletons appear but the moments (and causes) of death do not. In keeping with the "creature-features" that <u>Invasion</u> resembles, the alien unsheathes a yard-long green stinger, a "chitinous saber" dripping with poison, and stabs her. There is no doubt of her death, Hanlon says; the effect of the venom was "purely academic" (176). Yet in the final chapter, she is not dead. The aliens do not explain how they restored her; if Hanlon were intelligent, they state, he would already know (189).

Jack's "death" follows a similar pattern. Caught in the insanity of the Overlook, he attacks Wendy. She stabs him with a kitchen knife. "You bitch," Jack says, "You killed me" (400). Yet he is not truly dead either. "Jack" surfaces once more, when he confronts Danny on the third floor. Danny challenges the thing that was his father; Jack is restored long enough to look at Danny and reassert his love for his son.

The substantive differences between the two novels imply a generic shift. Timberlake Farm is not evil; the house is not haunted. In spite of surface similarities to the Overlook, it merely provides a backdrop for the plot: alien invasion. The Overlook, on the other hand, focuses the horror; it is haunted, the ultimate haunted house, controlled by its own desires and lusts rather than by ectoplasmic remnants of former inhabitants.

Science fiction into horror . . . if King had written *Invasion*, the shift of genres would explain most of the structural and thematic differences between *Invasion* and *The Shining*. The latter is more complex, a finer achievement by any standard. Even its structure demonstrates greater finesse. *Invasion* is straight-line, first-person narrative. *The Shining* inter-weaves simultaneous actions and perceptions, shifting from character to character as parts blend in the reader's mind to create the whole. In "On The Shining," King refers to his original conception of *The Shining* as a five-act Shakespearean tragedy, an idea he admits was pretentious yet fundamental to what he hoped to achieve.

In the context of King's fiction, including *'Salem's Lot* and *The Shining*, *Rage*, *The Long Walk* and *Roadwork*, *Invasion* shares a number of traits. It is not surprising that some readers might have seen his hand in the novel, especially in light of the furor generated by the Bachman revelation. None of the similarities seems definitive, however; there is not enough evidence to assert that King wrote *Invasion*.

On the other hand, at least two pieces of evidence militate against King as author of *Invasion*.

First, King has denied using "Aaron Wolfe" as a pseudonym. In addition, he has never referred to "Aaron Wolfe" in his other works, as he mentions "John Swithen" in *Carrie* (but then, nowhere does he refer to "Richard Bachman," either). The obituary for Richard Bachman in *Castle Rock* (#5, 2) mentioned two survivors: Bachman's wife, Claudia Inez; and a half-brother, John Swithen. None of the other possible pseudonyms were included.

And second, not only has King denied authorship, but at least one research scholar and horror-fantasy bibliographer has attributed the "Aaron Wolfe" pseudonym to a writer other than King. The Guide to SF in LC Classification mentions neither "Eth Natas" nor "Richard Bachman," but does identify "Wolfe." While the identity of "Aaron Wolfe" is not widely known (and he apparently prefers it so), there is sufficient evidence, both bibliographic and stylistic, to link Invasion to one of King´s contemporaries, also best known as a writer of supernatural horror; his recent novels, in fact, share many characteristics with King´s novels, creating a partially justifiable sense that King might have written Invasion.

Thus, while internal evidence is sufficiently intriguing to keep speculations alive, it is (to borrow Stephanie Leonard´s phrase) "safe to say" that King did not write Invasion, Exorcism, or any of the other novels sometimes attributed to him. Since February 9, 1985, the question of who wrote Rage, The Long Walk, Roadwork, The Running Man and Thinner has been resolved. In spite of lingering suggestions to the contrary, all evidence indicates that we now have access to King´s full canon to date.

King himself was surprised when the Bachman pseudonym created so much excitement. Initially, he chose to publish under a pen-name merely as a means to get works in print that might otherwise not have been published. Publishers are reluctant to bring out more than one title a year by a writer as popular as King; as a result, he has generally run several books ahead. A pen-name seemed the best alternative. The name "Richard Bachman" was not planned; originally Rage was submitted under the name Guy Pillsbury, but withdrawn when word leaked out that it was actually by King.

Perhaps another "Richard Bachman" will not be necessary for King. He has published The Talisman and The Eyes of the Dragon within months of each other, with no ill effects on either as far as sales or popularity. Having six film versions of his stories appear within a year has not resulted in any noticable drop in sales. Since King is working on an arrangement to publish four novels under his own name in either 1986 or 1987, future pseudonyms may be unnecessary.

Still, "Bachman" has been a great boost for King. It has brought his name as much (if not more) attention in some circles as his other novels. It has allowed him to work outside supernatural horror at a time when he was virtually type-cast. In return, King has shown a good deal of affection for "Bachman." <u>Thinner</u> is still listed under Bachman's name, even when posters glaring from the bookstore walls announce that King wrote the novel. "I'd like to see <u>Thinner</u> sold aggressively," he has said, "because I'd want that for Dick's last book" (Brown, C2).

Richard Bachman might be dead, but his books are doing well. Four will be re-issued in the fall. Two, <u>The Long Walk</u> and <u>The Running Man</u>, have film options. And one has made it to the top of the bestsellers lists (King originally hoped for Bachman eventually to make it on his own, perhaps after another novel or so).

All in all, it's not a bad record for a one-time merchant seaman, part-time dairy farmer from New Hampshire.

Appendix

THE BACHMAN NOVELS--SYNOPSES

I. Rage

A high-school student, Charlie Decker, shoots his algebra teacher, then holds the class hostage. Using an intercom, the principal, the school counselor, and the head of the Maine State Police try to persuade him to surrender; he turns the game on them by threatening to shoot his hostages.

In the meantime, the class, led by Charlie's reminiscences of his family life, opens up. The atmosphere in the classroom shifts from fear to psychological freedom for the students. Eventually, they gain enough understanding of themselves, their parents, and the adult world to turn on the one student who epitomizes that world, Ted Jones.

Charlie decides to release the hostages at 1:00, provided he and the students remain undisturbed for the last hour. During that hour, they complete their individual narratives and verbally and physically attack Ted Jones. At the stated time, Charlie releases the class. The students leave, except Ted Jones, who is in a nearly catatonic state. The authorities burst in and shoot Charlie. In a series of brief chapters, King summarizes the conditions of Ted Jones, the other students, and Charlie Decker.

II: The Long Walk

Ray Garraty and 99 other boys begin the nonstop Long Walk from northern Maine toward Boston. They are accompanied by armed guards and halftracks equipped to monitor the boys' speed and direction. If a Walker does not continue forward at four miles per hour, he receives a Warning. After three Warnings, the Walker is shot. The Walk ends when only one boy remains alive and moving. He receives The Prize: anything he wants for the rest of his life.

 <u>The Long Walk</u> details the shifting relationships among the boys by means of conversations, internal monologues, and narratives of the boys´ deaths.

III: <u>Roadwork</u>

 The city decides to build a freeway spur that will demolish Barton George Dawes´ home and the place he has worked for twenty years, the Blue Ribbon Laundry. Dawes postpones finding either a new home or a new site for the laundry until it is too late. He loses his wife and his job, and lives alone in the house where his son had died several years before. Increasingly isolated, he meets a young hitchhiker and spends the night with her; later, he approaches an underground armament dealer and tries to buy explosives. When the dealer refuses, Dawes makes his own explosives and blows up several pieces of equipment and the site office, delaying construction several months. Impressed by Dawes´ independence, the dealer sells him the explosives.

 Dawes arranges to remain in his home until the last possible day. In the meantime, he sends money to his wife and to the young hitchhiker, settles all of his private matters, and prepares to meet the authorities when they come to take possession of his house.

IV: <u>The Running Man</u>

 Benjamin Richards lives with his wife and daughter in Co-op City, a slum in the America of 2025. He is unemployed; his wife prostitutes herself to earn money for their desperately ill child. As a last resort, Richards becomes a contestant on <u>The Running Man</u>, a television game show on which contestants must survive for one month. The prize is a billion dollars, but no one has yet lived more than eight days without being killed either by citizens or by the Network's team of hunters.

Richards begins his run, moving northward into Maine and meeting an underground dedicated to making public the government's disregard for human welfare. As Richards finds new hiding places, his involvement with the underground increases and the Network hunters draw nearer.

He kidnaps a housewife and forces her to drive him to an airfield, where he extorts a jet from the authorities. Safely in the air, Richards arranges his final confrontation with the Hunters and with the Network.

V: Thinner

Billy Halleck, an overweight lawyer, kills an old gypsy woman in a car accident. At the hearing, Halleck has been absolved of any guilt. The woman's father, however, seeks his own justice on Halleck and others. Halleck begins losing weight; the judge grows scales; the police chief develops a hideous skin condition. While Halleck's wife, doctor, and friends worry about cancer, Halleck becomes convinced that he has been cursed. He leaves home, trailing the gypsies through New England, finally discovering their camp and confronting the old man.

When the gypsy refuses to remove the curse, Halleck calls on the one man he can trust, a New York mobster named Ginelli. Ginelli becomes Halleck's own curse, intimidating the old man into showing Halleck how to transfer the curse. The curse under his control, Halleck attempts his own brand of justice, with horrible results.

LIST OF WORKS CITED

"Bachman Revealed to be Stephen King Alias," Publishers Weekly 22 March 1985: 43.

Barron, Neil. "´Bachman´ Indeed Reads Like Stephen King." Fantasy Review (March 1985): 15.

Bellows, Keith. "The King of Terror" (Interview). Sourcebook: The Magazine for Seniors. 1982: 33.

Bradbury, Ray. Fahrenheit 451. New York: Ballantine, 1953.

Brown, Stephen. "Stephen King, Shining Through." Washington Post 9 April 1985: C1-C2.

Campbell, Ramsey, ed. New Tales of the Cthulhu Mythos. Sauk City WI: Arkham House, 1980.

Castle Rock: The Stephen King Newsletter. Ed. Stephanie Leonard. Issues #1 (January 1985), #2 (February 1985), #3 (March 1985), #4 (April 1985).

Collins, Bob. "Weinberg Gets Last Laugh." Fantasy Review 77 (March 1985): 15.

Delany, Samuel. "Some Reflections on SF Criticism." Science-Fiction Studies, 25 (November 1981): 233-239.

Fantasy Mongers 13 (Winter 1984/1985): 5. Review of Winter´s The Art of Darkness.

---------- 13 (Winter 1984/1985): 5. Review of Thinner.

Ferguson, Mary. "Strawberry Spring: Stephen King´s Gothic Universe." Footsteps V (April 1985): 50-55.

Fiedler, Leslie. "Fantasy as Commodity, Pornography, Camp and Myth," *Fantasy Review* 68 (June 1984): 6-9,42.

Gareffa, Peter M. "Stephen King." *Contemporary Authors*, New Revision Series, I. 333-336.

Golding, William. *The Lord of the Flies*. New York: Coward-McCann, 1955.

Graham, Mark. "Fit for a King," *Rocky Mountain News* 23 December 1984: 26M.

Grant, Charles L. "Introduction" to *Shadows*. Ed. Charles Grant. New York: Berkley, 1980. 7-10.

Gray, Paul. "Master of Postliterate Prose." *Time* 20 August 1982: 87.

Hatlen, Burton. "The Destruction and Re-Creation of the Human Community in Stephen King's *The Stand*." *Footsteps V* (April 1985): 56-60.

---------- "The Mad Dog and Maine." In *Shadowings*. Ed. Douglas Winter. Mercer Island WA: Starmont House, 1983, 33-37.

Hemingway, Ernest. *In Our Time*. New York: Scribner's, 1958. [Rpt. of 1925 ed.]

---------- *The Nick Adams Stories*. New York: Scribner's, 1972.

Jackson, Rosemary. *Fantasy: The Literature of Subversion*. New York: Methuen, 1981.

Jackson, Shirley. "The Lottery." In *The Lottery and Other Stories*. New York: Farrar, Straus, Giroux, 1982. 291-302.

"King's Too Fast For His Own Good." *Los Angeles Daily News* 11 April 1985: 26.

King, Stephen. "The Blue Air Compressor." Onan (January 1971): 70-78; rpt. in Heavy Metal (July 1981): 31-33.

---------- "Cain Rose Up." In Skeleton Crew. New York: Putnam's, 1985. Rpt. from Ubris (Spring 1968): 175-180.

---------- Carrie. Garden City: Doubleday (n.d.; Book Club Edition). [Orig. publ. Doubleday, 1974]

---------- Christine. New York: Viking, 1983.

---------- "Crouch End." In New Tales of the Cthulhu Mythos. Ed. Ramsey Campbell. Sauk City WI: Arkham House, 1980. 5-32.

---------- Cujo. New York: Viking, 1981.

---------- Cycle of the Werewolf. New York: Signet, 1985. [Rpt of 1983 ltd. ed.]

---------- Danse Macabre. New York: Everest, 1981.

---------- Different Seasons. New York: Viking Press, 1982.

---------- "Do The Dead Sing?" Yankee. November 1981: 139-143, 238ff.

---------- "Dr. Seuss & The Two Faces of Fantasy." Fantasy Review, 68 (June 1984): 10-12.

---------- "Gramma." Weirdbook, 19 (Spring 1984): 3-16.

---------- "Graveyard Shift." In Night Shift. New York: New American Library, 1979. 35-51.

---------- "Here There Be Tygers." In Skeleton Crew. New York: Putnam's, 1985. 135-140. Rpt. from Ubris (Spring 1968).

---------- "King's Garbage Truck." The Maine Campus 6 March 1969: 9. [Column in the university newspaper from 20 February 1969 to 21 May 1970.]

---------- The Long Walk (as Richard Bachman). New York: New American Library, 1979.

---------- "The Mangler." In Night Shift. New York: Signet, 1979. 74-92.

---------- "The Mist." In Dark Forces. Ed. Kirby McCauley. New York: Bantam, 1981. 1-130. [Orig. publ. Viking, 1980]

---------- "My High School Horrors." Sourcebook: The Magazine for Seniors. 1982: 30-33.

---------- "Nona." In Shadows. Ed. Charles L. Grant. New York: Berkley, 1980. 187-223.

---------- Pet Sematary. Garden City: Doubleday, 1983.

---------- Rage (as Richard Bachman). London: New English Library, 1983. [Rpt. of New American Library 1977 ed.]

---------- Roadwork (as Richard Bachman). London: New English Library, 1981. [Rpt. of New American Library 1981 ed.]

---------- The Running Man (as Richard Bachman). London: New English Library, 1983. [Rpt. of New American Library 1982 ed.]

---------- "Sometimes They Come Back." In Night Shift. New York: Signet, 1979. 143-170.

---------- The Stand. Garden City: Doubleday (n.d., Book Club Edition). [Orig. publ. Doubleday, 1978]

---------- "Strawberry Spring." In Night Shift.

New York: Signet, 1979. 171-180.

---------- "Suffer The Little Children." <u>Cavalier</u> (February 1972): 35-36, 38, 90, 92, 94.

---------- <u>Thinner</u> (as Richard Bachman). New York: New American Library, 1984.

---------- and Peter Straub. <u>The Talisman</u>. New York: Viking/Putnam's, 1984

Knight, Damon. "What is Science Fiction?" In <u>Turning Points.</u> Ed. Damon Knight. New York: Harper & Row, 1977. 62-69.

Leonard, Stephanie. Letter to Michael Collings. 2 April 1985.

Lovecraft, H. P. "The Colour Out of Space." In <u>The Colour Out of Space</u>. New York: Lancer, 1964. 7-35.

---------- "The Picture in the House." In <u>Fantastic Worlds</u>. Ed. Eric S. Rabkin. New York: Oxford University Press, 1979. 257-265.

---------- "The Rats in the Walls." In <u>Great Tales of Terror and the Supernatural</u>. Ed. Herbert A. Wise and Phyllis Fraser. New York: Modern Library, 1944. 1010-1031.

McDowell, Edwin. "Behind the Best Sellers." <u>New York Times Book Review</u> 27 September 1981: 40.

Modderno, Craig. "I'd Really Like to Write a Rock'n'Roll Novel." <u>USA Today</u> 10 May 1985.

Montgomery, Constance Cappell. <u>Hemingway in Michigan</u>. New York: Fleet, 1966.

Poe, Edgar Allan. "The Black Cat." In <u>Fantastic Worlds</u>. Ed. Eric S. Rabkin. New York: Oxford University Press, 1979. 247-256.

Proch, Paul and Charles Kaufman. "Eggboiler." *National Lampoon*, 2 (May 1984): 32-37, 48, 54, 70.

Singer, Loren. *The Parallax View*. Garden City: Doubleday, 1970.

Slung, Michelle. "Scare Tactics." *New York Times Book Review* 10 May 1981: 15, 27.

Smith, Joan H. "Pseudonym Kept Five King Novels a Mystery." *Bangor Daily News* 9 Feb. 1985.

Stewart, Robert. "The Rest of King." *Starship* (Spring 1981): 45-46. Continuation of an interview published in *Heavy Metal*, January, February, March 1981.

Underwood, Tim and Chuck Miller. *Fear Itself: The Horror Fiction of Stephen King*. New York: Plume/New American Library, 1984. [Rpt. of Underwood-Miller 1982 ed.]

Winter, Douglas, "The Art of Darkness." In *Shadowings*. Ed. Douglas Winter. Mercer Island WA: Starmont House, 1983. 3-23.

---------- "Stephen King, Peter Straub & The Quest for *The Talisman*." *Twilight Zone* (January/February 1985): 62-68.

---------- *Stephen King: The Art of Darkness*. New York: New American Library, 1984.

Young, Philip. *Ernest Hemingway*. University Park PA: Pennsylvania State University Press, 1966.

Zagorski, Edward J. *Teacher's Manual: The Novels of Stephen King*. New York: New American Library, 1981.

SELECTIVE INDEX OF NAMES AND TITLES

And Justice For All
  (film): 129
"Apt Pupil": 137
Babylon Here: 71
Bandler, Michael: 50
Barron, Neil: 116-118,
  138
"Battleground": 90
"Beachworld": 94-95
"Big Wheels: A Story of
  the Laundry Game":
  90, 143
Blackwood, Algernon: 11
Bloch, Robert: 13
"The Blue Air Compres-
  sor": 5, 26, 90
Blue Ribbon Laundry:
  15, 32, 79, 84, 90
"The Body": 74, 137,
  143
Bradbury, Ray: 49-50,
  101-102, 105, 114
Brain From Planet Arous
  (film): 89
"The Breathing Method":
  141
Brown, Stephen: 2
"Cain Rose Up": 21, 41
Carrie: 3, 5, 8, 14,
  16, 21, 22-23, 25,
  28, 30-34, 42, 47,
  67-68, 70-72, 90-92,
  102, 106, 125,
  143-145, 151
Carroll, Lewis: 73, 99
Castle Rock: 3, 23, 68,
  72, 119, 138, 139,
  151
Cat´s Eye (film): 106

"Children of the Corn":
  142, 143
Children of the Corn
  (film): 106
Christine: 4, 6, 40,
  62, 121-122, 125,
  143
Collins, Robert: 1, 139
Conrad, Joseph: 50-51
Creepshow: 4, 11, 49
"Crouch End": 13
Cujo: 4, 14, 19, 47,
  72, 74, 78, 96, 106,
  109, 120, 121, 125,
  132, 143
Currey, Lloyd: 1, 116
Cycle of the Werewolf:
  4, 81, 143
Danse Macabre: 4, 51,
  52, 59, 95, 132, 146
The Dark Tower: The
  Gunslinger: 4, 5,
  139, 140
The Day The Earth Stood
  Still (film): 146
The Dead Zone: 4, 70,
  114, 125, 143
Delany, Samuel R.: 96
Different Seasons: 4,
  9, 13, 74, 106, 121,
  137
"Do the Dead Sing?":
  14, 121
"Dolan´s Cadillac": 68,
  130
Dos Passos, John: 73
Eliot, T. S.: 73
The Eyes of the Dragon:
  4, 53, 143, 149, 152

Exorcism ("Eth Natas"): 138, 140-142, 152
The Exorcist (film): 23
Faulkner, William: 74
Fiedler, Leslie: 5-6
"The Fifth Quarter" ("John Swithen"): 7
Firestarter: 4, 52, 72, 77, 125, 143
Frost, Robert: 99
"Garbage Truck": See "King's Garbage Truck"
Getting It On (Rage): 44-46, 71, 102, 103
Golding, William: The Lord of the Flies 33, 39, 50
Graham, Mark: 116-117, 126
"Gramma": 17, 26, 143
Grant, Charles: 9-10
"Graveyard Shift": 13
Gray, Paul: 106-108, 137
Hatlen, Burton: 15, 46-47, 69
Hemingway, Ernest: 73, 74-77, 83-85, 88, 99, 135; "Big Two-Hearted River" 75-77, 80, 89
"Here There Be Tygers": 21
"I Am the Doorway": 94-95
"I Know What You Need": 142, 143
Invasion (Aaron Wolfe): 138-139, 142-152
Jackson, Rosemary: 12
Jackson, Shirley: 11, 14, 52-55, 135; "The Lottery" 39, 52-56
Jaws (film): 23

Kafka, Franz: 73, 90
"King's Garbage Truck": 28, 91-92, 98
Knight, Damon: 93-94
Kornbluth, C.C.: 101
L'amour, Louis: 135
"The Last Rung": 137
"The Ledge": 106, 131
Leiber, Fritz: 13
Leonard, Stephanie: 71, 138, 139, 141
Levin, Ira: 11
Long, Frank Belknap: 13
The Long Walk: 2, 3, 14-19, 21-23, 46-69, 70-72, 75, 79, 89-90, 93, 97-98, 104-106, 109-111, 114, 122, 134, 135, 137, 141, 143, 146, 151, 152, 155-156
Lovecraft, H. P.: 10-11, 13-14, 49, 73, 89, 120-121
Love Lessons ('John Wilson'): 8, 139
"The Man Who Would Not Shake Hands": 141
"Man With a Belly": 90, 130
"The Mangler": 15, 32, 90, 117
Manuel, Richard A: 3
Matheson, Richard: 11, 14
Miller, Walter: 115
Modderna, Craig: 7
"The Monkey": 5
Montgomery, Constance: 79-80
"Mrs. Todd's Shortcut": 143
"My High School Horrors": 20, 33
Natas, Eth (pseud.):

166

138
Night Shift: 4, 7, 47, 146
"Night Surf": 94-95
"Nona": 11-14
Orwell, George: 73, 99-101, 105, 114
Pet Sematary: 4, 122, 125, 131, 149
Poe, Edgar Allan: 10-13, 42, 49, 73, 89, 120
Pohl, Frederik: 101
Psycho (film): 33
"The Raft": 5, 81, 134, 143
Rage: 2, 3, 14, 16, 17, 20-45, 46, 48, 52, 59, 61, 62, 65-66, 67-68, 70, 72-75, 79, 84, 89-90, 93, 103, 109-111, 128, 137, 142, 143, 146, 151, 152-155
Reagan, Ronald: 80-81
"Rita Hayworth and Shawshank Redemption": 137
Roadwork: 2, 3, 15-18, 22, 46, 70-91, 93, 99, 109, 117, 130, 134, 135, 137, 141-143, 146, 151-152, 156
The Running Man: 2, 3, 15-18, 59-60, 71, 79, 86, 89-90, 92-114, 119, 122, 128, 134, 135, 137, 140, 143, 152, 156-157
´Salem´s Lot: 4, 70, 71, 81, 125, 143, 145-151
Shakespeare, William: 73, 99
Shelley, Mary: 10
The Shining: 4, 13, 16, 18, 19, 42, 52, 70, 81, 123, 125, 141, 143, 144-146, 148-151
Singer, Loren: The Parallax View 44, 45, 102-103
Skeleton Crew: 3
"Slade": 139, 140
Smith, Clark Ashton: 13
Smith, Joan: 22, 46
"Sometimes They Come Back": 21
"The Star Invaders": 89, 94
The Stand: 4, 35-36, 47, 48, 70, 72, 81, 95, 114, 115, 125, 141, 143
Stevenson, R. L.: 11
Stewart, Robert: 44, 71
Stoker, Bram: 11
Straub, Peter: 3, 4, 6, 11, 73, 80; Shadowland 73
"Strawberry Spring": 21, 142
"Stud City": 74
"Suffer the Little Children": 21
Sullivan, Jack: 123
Swithen, John (pseud. for Stephen King): 7, 35, 138, 151
Sword in the Darkness: 71
The Talisman: 3-6, 73, 80-81, 92, 106, 118-119, 124, 135-137, 142, 149, 152
Thinner: 1, 4-7, 9,

15-19, 49, 71, 90, 92, 115-137, 138, 142-144, 152, 157
Thompson, Bill: 13, 102
The Tommyknockers: 140
Tolkien, J.R.R.: 27, 51
Underwood, Tim and Chuck Miller: Fear Itself 47
Vonnegut, Kurt: 73
"The Wedding Gig": 90, 130
Weinberg, Bob and Phyllis: 1,
Wells, H.G.: 10, 99-100
Wilde, Oscar: 11
Wilder, Thornton: 50
Wilson, John (pseud.): 8, 139
Winter, Douglas: 3, 4, 6, 9, 14, 43, 46-47, 68, 69, 71, 80, 102, 115, 116, 122
"The Woman in the Room": 137
Young, Philip: 74-75
Zagorski, Edward J.: 11,

```
813 K54 Zc-s Me.Coll.
Collings, Michael R.
Stephen King as Richard
   Bachman
```

WITHDRAWN

PORTLAND PUBLIC LIBRARY
5 MONUMENT SQ.
PORTLAND, ME 04101

DATE DUE			
APR 15 1992			
DEC 13 1994			
MAR 03 1995			
APR 26 1995			
AUG 02 1995			
MAR 25 1997			
APR 15 1997			